TEACHING SHAKESPEARE ON SCREEN

"The Film's the Thing"

EDITED BY

NEIL E. BÉCHERVAISE

WRITTEN BY

NEIL E. BÉCHERVAISE, JOE BELANGER,
BILL DAVISON, JODIE MCFADDEN,
DENNIS ROBINSON, SARAH TAINTON,
AND KEN WATSON

Pacific Educational Press
Vancouver Canada

ISBN 1-895766-64-8

Pacific Educational Press
Faculty of Education
University of British Columbia
6365 Biological Sciences Rd.
Vancouver, Canada V6T 1Z4
Telephone: (604) 822-5385
Facsimile: (604) 822-6603
e-mail: pep@interchange.ubc.ca
www.pep.educ.ubc.ca

This work was originally published in Australia in 1999 by St Clair Press Pty Ltd. of Sydney as *Shakespeare on Celluloid* ISBN 0-949898-90-2. This North American edition is published with the agreement of St. Clair Press and is an enlargement of the original work.

National Library of Canada Cataloguing in Publication Data

Main entry under title:

Teaching Shakespeare on screen

Previously published as: Shakespeare on celluloid.
Includes bibliographical references and index.
ISBN 1-895766-64-8

1. Shakespeare, William, 1564-1616--Film and video adaptations. 2. English drama--Film and video adaptations. I. Bichervaise, Neil E. II. Title: Shakespeare on celluloid.

PR3093.T42 2001   791.43'6   C2001-911305-6

Acknowledgements

The editor and authors wish to acknowledge the assistance of their students from primary and secondary classrooms and university lecture halls in Australia and Canada whose enthusiasm for reading and film viewing have made this book a reality. For their assistance with additional research, development, and classroom testing of materials for this text, the authors wish to express their particular thanks to Sehan Nas and Prue Greene from the University of Sydney, Australia, and to Leanne Fukui, Peter Hill, Michael Lattimer, Michelle Porter, and David L. Young for their enthusiastic work in the summer of 1997 at the University of British Columbia, Canada.

The publisher acknowledges the support of the Government of Canada through the Book Publishing Industry Development Program (BPIDP) for its publishing activities.

Design: Warren Clark
Printed and bound in Canada
04 03 02 01   5 4 3 2 1

Contents

Foreword

This book uses and expands on reader response theory as a theoretical base. Essentially, this means that we believe that film viewers/readers bring a unique set of experiences and understandings to their reading of a film and construct the "text" by applying these understandings to the reading. To the extent that the readers, experience, and knowledge are individual, each of their readings is unique.

But that is too haphazard for us as teachers. We want students to feel confident in coming to grips with the text as informed and critically resistant readers who "know the rules of the game" of reading film as well as we expect them to know the "rules" for reading literature. Otherwise, what is the point of being an educator?

As writers, we bring our own research into the films and a collective range of film-watching experiences that is far more extensive than that of the average film reader. We also bring the language, the grammar, and the ability to contextualize which we model for students and beginning film readers. Without such modelling, they have no framework upon which to build and against which to confirm their own developing facility as film readers.

Shakespeare was a commercial playwright and a theatre owner. He was in business to get crowds through the doors. He developed a new tragedy and a new comedy each season. If things worked, he ran with them. He was commercial first. As such, we believe, he would have been a film producer/director in the 1990s—perhaps in the style of Kenneth Branagh with his ensemble approach to film-making (for example, in *Peter's Friends*), perhaps in the manner of Spielberg with his wide range of interests in universal issues. Film is the twenty-first century medium. How should we/can we read it? This, for us, is what the book is about.

In this book we explore the range of translations of Shakespearean play-texts which have been made on film. We have focussed on the readily available films and refer in passing to others we know but which may not be readily accessible.

To some extent, the approaches to the films are individualistic but we have endeavoured to meld them into a stylistically coherent structure. Each chapter is written as a discussion supplemented by activities, observations, and asides which extend and help to fill, for some students, what may otherwise remain as silences.

Neil E. Béchervaise

Establishing Shot

Umberto Eco (1979) proposed that "critically resistant reading" was essential for readers to avoid being "positioned" by the author in such a way that they could be manipulated into accepting unreasonable or unacceptable interpretations of events. Bertoldt Brecht's refusal to allow his audience to engage as mere passive spectators predates Eco's work. Most filmmakers foster and even presume unthinking, non-critical acceptance of their interpretations. Branagh's two-hour cut of his four-hour *Hamlet* forces its consideration, however.

The Structure of the Book

This book is divided into five parts. Part I examines the relationship between audience and performance, leading to an exploration of the differences between reading literature, play-texts, and films. Parts II–V identify the elements most commonly underpinning effective storytelling for entertainment: narration, spatial relationships, sequentiality, and closure.

It is presumed that our readers will find many examples of every storytelling element in each of the films. Consequently, there is no need to follow the book's order of presentation or to use only those films discussed in each section to substantiate the focus of that section. Keen film readers will wish to add films not mentioned, or to replace films mentioned with others which seem more appropriate or appealing. We encourage this approach and wish we had more space to add extra films that we have reluctantly omitted.

The headnotes for each part have been written to stand alone. Readers wishing to apply film-reading principles to films other than Shakespearean translations will find them a useful organizing guide in the development of critical film readership.

Each chapter contains:

- **Establishing Shots**: focussing information directed towards the fundamental concepts involved in the chapter.
- **Key Shots**: essential definitional information.
- **Cutaways**: student activities that lead from lower-order, individually-focussed information retrieval that depends on students' prior knowledge and establishes a shared knowledge base; that is, they establish an entry knowledge profile for each individual student.
- **Director's Cuts**: higher-order activities promoting sharing of knowledge and processes to ensure comprehension and to promote categorization, analysis, synthesis, and informed surmise.

The Play-Text as a Recipe for Action

Wherever possible, the authors have avoided attention to the text of the plays by omitting annotated references to particular scenes or lines. We accept that this may annoy those who see the films as impure versions of literary works. However, we believe that the films should be considered as translations of the plays to screen—as dynamic performances, in other words. Nevertheless, there are times when it is faster to reference the play than to spend hours rerunning the films to pinpoint a word or a sequence. In these cases, we have applied the generally accepted mode of notation, using capitalized Roman numerals to locate acts and lower case to identify scenes.

Audience and Performance

CHAPTER ONE

Reading Film as Text

Establishing Shot 1

The authors of this book agree that film viewing is a form of reading. To read effectively, we need to know the vocabulary, the grammar, and the conventions used in constructing the text we are reading. We also need to understand the audience for whom the text is intended. Finally, we need to recognize the context in which the text is supposed to be read.

Establishing Shot 2

The idea of translation is useful in discussing the shift from literature to play to film because it clearly suggests that different "languages" are being used.

Film as a text differs from the literary text because it is written in movement, colour, and sound. It is designed to be read at a single sitting at a set pace. The pace of the reading is supposed to allow all readers to feel comfortable that they are reading at their own pace. As film readers, we usually only become conscious of the complexity of what we are watching when the film has been poorly written.

This text is designed to explore the ways in which films are constructed and the problems faced by film-makers who translate plays into film. Some of the questions film-makers have to answer include:

- How can the intention of the play-text be translated to film?
- Who will be the audience?
- How will the play-text need to be changed to suit the grammar and vocabulary of film?
- How will the play-text need to be changed to suit the historical and social context in which the play will be read?

As a means to understand the relation between the work of the playwright and of the film-maker, this text has also been designed to explore some of the central problems faced by playwrights:

- Who will be performing the play?
- Who will be in the audience?
- How will the play be performed?

In addressing these questions, it starts to become clear that the film-maker's concerns are remarkably similar to those of the playwright.

Translating Plays Into Film

The language of literature as we recognize it is the printed text. We are familiar with the complexities of grammar and vocabulary that characterize the effective use of this language. For most of us, as a result, reading the text means reading the words printed onto a succession of pages—each of which must be read before it is turned to reveal the next. Our literature reading allows us to read single words, phrases, and sections. We may pause, return, and even skip to establish a meaningful reading.

The play-text, however, is another language. It is intended to be seen (or heard) as the action of live players (actors) who will present an aural and/or visual text for us to "read." The players will not pause, stop, repeat, or skip sections of the play so that we can reflect or clarify our understanding of their text. Instead, working with the expanded vocabulary and grammar, or "language" of the play, they may add tonal variation, activity, colour, light, music, and sound effects to support and extend the meaning of their spoken text. Each of these elements assists us to read the play in a single performance, but the fact remains that what we cannot read in the performance cannot be repeated. We have no opportunity to return to line 53 or re-view Act II, scene ii to be sure that we understood what was being set up as a motivation for later action by the protagonist.

Film represents yet another language. Recorded for later transmission to an audience in the darkness and intimacy of a theatre on a large screen, the film is several steps removed from the literary text. The characters, the angles from which they are seen, their emotional relation to each other, the physical circumstances of their performance—each represents an alternative vocabulary and grammar which are selected and collected to present a single and singular reading of the text they present.

The apparent structures we translate from the screen cannot be the actual structures. We will not see the cameras, the lights, the director, the extras. We are not (at least we are not meant to be) conscious of the roles of the musicians, the editors, the colour matchers, the title designers, and the hundreds of others who support the "writing" of the film we read as a single text. The singularity of our reading of a film depends on the totality of its *constructedness*.

In the light of the theatre lobby, we recognize that we are about to see or have just seen a complex visual and aural construction. Inside the theatre, with the lights down and our attention focussed on the universe defined by the screen, we adopt a different set of semantic rules. We accept the "reality" of the screen universe and the context in which we are being entertained. We read the film as a specialized text.

The film-maker's intention is to devise a text for which there can only be one reading. The signs we recognize in literature or in a play performance may not signify the meanings we usually provide them with. Our literary training may be consciously turned against us to create new and more complex readings. Music may suggest impending disaster. Colour may create a sense of the romantic. Camera angles may confuse our reading of power relationships.

The basic intention of the commercial film-maker is to create an enter-

Establishing Shot 3

The film text is easily recognized as a postmodern construction: a complex series and sequence of intentions translated to film as if in a single reading.

tainment which will totally engage the interests and emotions of the audience. The elements of the film are woven together to create a seamless production in which music, dialogue, and images appear to have been created together. To develop a discriminating response as film readers, it becomes essential to understand the elements involved in the construction of the text. If we are to appreciate how the film achieves its purpose, we must teach ourselves to read against the intention of the film-maker.

The complexity of selecting carefully filmed and re-filmed shots from totally different sequences, composing music to reinforce this selection, adding sound effects, re-recording voices, correcting the colours to match the moods created, and then editing them into a finished film is a spectacular achievement—even for poor films. Film-makers create apparently seamless interpretations that are intended to be read in a single sitting. When they create films of Shakespearean plays, they make selections and generate interpretations that cannot be argued with during viewing. To create critical distance, film readers need to understand, in general terms, how films are made and, more importantly, why. The "why?" is rather obvious—to make money for their producers. Making money was a major concern for Shakespeare as a theatre owner too. The "how?" of film-making is also no secret. Many excellent "Making of . . ." films reveal the techniques and demystify the complexity of the industry. The role of teacher and student studying Shakespeare with the support of film productions is to keep this knowledge of the how and why of film-making at the forefront of thinking while we view the films. Resisting the temptation to be drawn in to the film as pure entertainment, we can review our responses, our interpretations, and our understanding within a critical framework. Using Eco's term, we can create a "critically resistant reading" of the film-maker's text. In doing so, we learn to create a critical framework from within which we translate the text into a meaningful and conscious reading.

Establishing Shot 4

Whether people speak or write or show pictures, they make choices about what to put in their message and what to leave out. The way they make their choice seems to be very simple, but every choice makes some things important and leaves other things out. Each choice includes some readers or viewers and excludes others.

Cutaway 1 Take 1

Remember an occasion when you were in one room and could hear a movie on television in another. How did you tell what was happening or about to happen? Was it possible to create a reasonably accurate image of what the scenery and even the actors' costumes looked like without seeing the screen?

Translating Shakespeare's Plays

Translating Shakespeare's plays into film presents particular problems:

- many people have strong feelings about Shakespeare because they once studied his plays at school;
- many ideas about how Shakespeare should be presented make it difficult to translate a Shakespearean play to film so that it satisfies both critics and more forgiving audiences;
- some people believe that because Shakespeare wrote in Elizabethan times, his plays must be presented historically.

The film translator of Shakespeare has to be both brave and talented to meet all the demands which will be made of the film.

The Intended Audience

When a text is written to be read as a piece of literature, the characters, settings, and events that fill the reader's mind must appear to present a reality according to the rules of reading. Some reading rules are related to the structure of written speech rather than spoken speech. Others are related to the way readers create a reality in their minds as they read.

Play-texts, however, are not usually written to be read as literature. They are more often written to be performed by actors on a stage. Readers expect to move from their homes to a performance area to watch the performance as audience members. Audience expectations may differ between individuals but the shared experience demands an interaction between players and audience. With words and action, staging, sets, lighting, costume, and make-up, the actors will create a performance for readers to share in. Readers will be expected to make adjustments between the reality of what they are seeing and the reality the actors are performing.

Film demands a more distanced reading. The film audience may move to a performance space but the actors, the settings, and the film-makers will not be there. Film must be read as if the performance space is shared between actors and audience. The reality of the film reader involves stepping through the screen into a world which has been created at another time and place.

Establishing Shot 5

The choice to read a novel, a play-text, or a film involves accepting a reality which is shared between the text and the reader but which only exists in the reader's mind.

Director's Cut 1

In Woody Allen's film *The Purple Rose of Cairo*, the hero of the film gets bored with playing the same role in every screening of the film and steps out of the screen while the film is being projected. Immediately, the film narrative is stopped as the characters on the screen, confused and then angry, try to decide what they can do without a hero. The audience for the film is equally confused and then angry. Discuss the restrictions we place on ourselves when we read a film and then decide whether the concept explored in films like *The Purple Rose of Cairo* or *Last Action Hero* provides us opportunities to consider our own role as audience.

Films are made according to rules of communication that are as strict as the spelling and grammar rules we use to write a story, an essay, or even a diary entry.

Cutaway 1 Take 2

Working in small groups, list some of the different things you have to believe when you watch a film, television series, or serial. Use this list to decide whether the news on television is more believable than a film that uses realistic characters in real settings.

When we go to see a film in a theatre, we expect comfortable seats and the lights to be turned out; we expect the film to be in focus and we expect to be able to hear the sound track. More importantly, we expect the film to make sense to us. If things happen that confuse us or that seem unreal within the story, we may argue that the film is of poor quality. If the style of the film does not follow the usual rules for film editing and composition then, again, we may argue that the film is of poor quality. We generally expect to see a film that follows rules we are already familiar with.

We expect characters to disappear from the screen so that we can see and hear other characters at different times and places or from different angles. We expect to hear music which heightens our understanding of the action and we expect to see colour or light and shade which match our previous understanding of how film is supposed to be. In fact, we already have a well developed understanding of the language of film.

Cutaway 1 Take 3

Have you ever watched the list of credits that comes at the end of a film? Who are all of the people who are involved in making a film? List some of the tasks which are credited in every film and group them according to whether they are most directly connected with the actors, the filming, the planning, the support of the film crew and actors, or the financing of the film.

Macbeth

Macbeth has been translated to film on a number of occasions but only two versions are readily available. Orson Welles directed and starred in the title role of his 1948 translation. Roman Polanski directed Jon Finch and Francesca Annis in a 1972 translation which was financed by Hugh Heffner (of *Playboy* fame) from a screenplay developed by Polanski and the English critic, Kenneth Tynan. The American gangster film, *Joe Macbeth*, provides some interesting interpretations of events in a less text-bound or historically bound setting.

Welles' *Macbeth* is essentially a vehicle for its star while the Polanski translation is unrelentingly violent, from the first scene with the witches through the bloody battle that opens the story to the final sequence in which Macbeth is beheaded and his head carried through the streets on a pike. This chapter will concentrate on the Polanski translation, which is the best known and most easily obtainable on videotape.

Ambition and a Touch of Witchcraft

A Shakespearean tragedy is created when one or several people in important roles have too much of an otherwise admirable characteristic. Romeo and Juliet loved wisely but not well. *Macbeth* is usually accepted as a tragedy of over-ambition. Like most of the lords of the time, probably, Macbeth would have been quite an acceptable king. He has an excellent reputation as a general; at the beginning of the play he has just saved King Duncan from certain defeat when the Thane of Cawdor turned traitor and sided with the king's enemies. He has been rewarded with that thane's title. It seems reasonable that he might, some day, become king. As a result, when he writes a letter to his wife, she accepts his dream of becoming king. However, she also recognizes that he is not politically ambitious enough to push himself towards the role. Instead, she develops a plan of her own: to kill the present king and install her husband in his place.

In Elizabethan times, to kill an annointed king was an appalling act, and Macbeth clearly recognizes this fact. Lady Macbeth, however, is more ambitious than her husband. She sweeps aside his arguments and demands that he "look like the innocent flower but be the serpent under it." Her role in the murder of King Duncan is central to the achievement of Macbeth's ambition, but she does not have to work alone.

The witches in Polanski's *Macbeth* are ugly and eccentric but they do not perform any particular magic. When Macbeth meets them and later follows them into their cave, he is fed a soup, "Double, double, toil and trouble, . . ." that causes him to hallucinate. He dreams that he is king. He dreams that he is unbeatable in battle. He also dreams several other images which he does not understand, or prefers not to accept, at the time. When he wakes, he is hung-over and the once-warm witches' cavern has become a cold, damp cave.

The witches allow Macbeth to play on his own ambitions and these weaken him to his wife's apparently more powerful ambition. However, just as she is about to murder Duncan because Macbeth will not, she discovers that he looks too much like her father. Despite her apparent ruthlessness—"Stop up the access and passage to remorse"—she cannot complete her own plan.

Macbeth recognizes that killing the king is a "deed of dreadful note" and when he has been pushed into the murder he accepts that "To know my deed 'twere best not know myself." His best friend Banquo recognizes the changes in his friend when he observes the apparent fulfilment of the witches' prophecies and soliloquizes "I fear thou play'dst most foully for 't."

Establishing Shot 2

Shortly after the Polish director Roman Polanski married young film star Sharon Tate, she was brutally murdered in a ritual occult-style killing by a group of followers of Charles Manson (who is still in jail for the crime). *Macbeth* is the first film directed by Polanski after this bloody ritual murder of his wife. The resulting film is particularly interesting for Polanski's treatment of the witches and for his use of violence.

Cutaway 2 Take 1

Lady Macbeth says that she has "given suck" but there is no evidence of children in either the original play-text or any of the filmed translations. From your developing knowledge of Elizabethan England, suggest how Lady Macbeth may have had children but has none now. Suggest how the possible loss of her children might affect Lady Macbeth's ambitions for her husband.

Casting and Translation

A comparative viewing of the first eight to ten minutes of both Polanski's and Welles' translations of *Macbeth* establishes that the cast ages are quite different. Since the story is about ambition and the role of the wife is central to the achievement of the ambition, different translations become possible with different cast ages. Similarly, the likely and possible influences on ambition change with age. Polanski's Macbeths are quite young (like himself and Sharon Tate perhaps?). In a modern world we might see Macbeth as a Wall Street stockbroker and his wife as a member of the New York social set. It would be difficult to see Orson Welles' Macbeth couple in such a translation.

The relative ages of kings and those who would like to be kings, of children as heirs to great power, and of acceptable lines of succession depend partly on personality and opportunity but possibly more on historical and cultural period. Shakespeare's *Macbeth*, like many of his plays, is a combination of fact and fiction where the fact is altered to suit the needs of entertainment for an audience familiar with the intrigues of the Elizabethan court.

Lady Macbeth and the Truth

Whether we read the play-text or a film text, our understanding of Lady Macbeth as the power behind the death of Duncan is likely to remain unchanged. What does change is the way we view Lady Macbeth's motivation for her emotional displays and for her various actions.

Polanski's casting of Francesca Annis as Lady Macbeth makes it difficult to dislike her. She is young, attractive, and well-groomed and -dressed. The camera first shows her at a distance and we hear her pleasant voice more clearly than we see her. But her response to Macbeth's letter and her subsequent actions leading to the murder of Duncan suggest that she is bitter and vicious. This is consistent with the distance Polanski provides and it makes a simple classification of her actions difficult. She seems to be in the background, directing the action rather than taking part.

Lady Macbeth's eventual breakdown and death seem inconsistent with her early strength but we rarely see her in close-up. She delivers significant soliloquies but they are often overheard from a distance—for example, by the physician. The only clues we have about Lady Macbeth's real nature are inconsistent and incomplete. She is quick to recognize opportunity, both from the letter and from her plan for Duncan; she is ambitious for her husband; she appears to be bitter and ruthless as she expresses her wish to be more like a man, "stop up the access and passage to remorse," and willing to dash out the brains of her child to achieve her purpose, "pluck'd my nipple from his boneless gums, /And dash'd the brains out." On the other hand, she cannot kill Duncan when she has the opportunity because he reminds her of her father and she is ultimately overcome by the blood on her hands: "Out, damned spot! out, I say." Before her death we see her at an extreme distance and completely nude—revealed in every detail but too distant to be understood.

The role of Lady Macbeth is never clarified in Polanski's translation. She has power over her husband but it is not sufficient to hold him in control of the throne. She may be wicked, cruel, and even responsible for the tragedy but Polanski never allows us close enough to see more than her grace and beauty when she is acting the gracious hostess before the assassination. We might see Lady Macbeth as evil but the king never can.

Cutaway 2 Take 4

Dressed in blue and white, Lady Macbeth wears the colours of the Madonna. Discuss the different ways in which Polanski suggests Lady Macbeth's gentleness and loving nature while shifting the appearance of evil intentions to her husband.

Compare your reading of the film with your reading of the relevant scenes in the play. Has Polanski created a fair translation of Lord and Lady Macbeth?

We are reminded of the witches' words, "Fair is foul and foul is fair . . ." and of Duncan's observation of Cawdor. Nothing is as it appears and since it is not possible to see what people are really thinking, trust is a real problem. Shakespeare had already explored this theme more fully in *Richard III*. Polanski suggests it more completely in his presentation of the relationship between Malcolm and Donalbain. The final scene showing Donalbain seeking the witches suggests that he will follow Macbeth's path in seeking to be king in place of his own brother. We cannot foresee the future but Polanski, as director, suggests that it repeats itself.

Cutaway 2 Take 5

Cawdor dies brutally but bravely. Polanski and Tynan provide him with dying words, "Long live the king." Malcolm and Donalbain are confused but Duncan dismisses them with the statement, "There's no art to find the mind's construction in the face." Compare this treatment with Orson Welles' translation of the same sequence. Which is the more powerful sequence? How does Welles' translation assist in our understanding of Malcolm and Donalbain in ways which Polanski omits?

"Yon castle hath an pleasant seat"

Writing the screenplay for a film requires two major elements: a clear idea of how the intention of the original text will be translated to the screen; and a careful selection of the original textual elements which are essential to the screen translation.

Most of us have a clear cultural base for picturing a castle. If we come from cultures with strong literary links to Britain, we are probably familiar with the kinds of castles English kings and queens lived in—from the outside at least.

If we come from non-British cultures, we may see castles completely differently. Akiro Kurosawa's Japanese translation of *Macbeth* onto film, *Throne of Blood,* follows the play-text quite accurately but the castles are made of timber. They would not have been out of place in Canada a century ago. Castles and fortresses in Pakistan or India are different again, in both shape and size. Some Scottish castles are small: protected homes rather than turreted fortresses. To film the Macbeth castle, Polanski found an existing castle in Wales.

Stormy Weather

Though Shakespeare's audience would have been satisfied with the description of the birds flying in and out of the turrets of the Macbeth castle, Polanski and Tynan have omitted its description in place of a visual "reality." In making this decision, they have taken the opportunity to replace a scene of dialogue with a visual procession. When Duncan first sees the Macbeth castle, it is bathed in sunlight and looks quite welcoming. As the royal procession advances, clouds gather and as the castle gates are thrown open to welcome the king, rain begins to fall and people scurry for shelter. A fierce storm blows into the festivities of the banquet held in Duncan's honour that evening and the shutters have to be locked to keep out the fury of the storm. It is worthwhile comparing this omission of a complete scene with Welles' treatment of the same scene.

Links between the weather, which was believed to be controlled by the gods, and human events are quite common metaphors in literature. Their linking seems to be quite natural. We enjoy pleasant events in pleasant weather. A picnic in a storm is not likely to create fond memories. The storm over the Macbeth castle sets the atmosphere for the murder. Just before Duncan arrives, we see Lady Macbeth at a distance on the battlements with the sun behind her and her hair flying in the wind. The storm over the witches' cave follows the execution of the opposing army at the beginning of the story. Macbeth seeks the witches in darkness, and fog has hidden the witches in the Polanski prologue. Later, Macbeth will be crowned in sunlight but it will be the last sunny day to be shown. In the end, Donalbain will repeat Macbeth's visit to the witches in wind and rain.

Cutaway 2 Take 6

From your viewing of the Welles translation, identify the sequences in which weather and natural setting are used to heighten or parallel emotional mood or literal meaning. Compare these with Polanski's treatment and suggest which translation makes the more powerful symbolic use of nature.

Lady Macbeth looks like an Amazon on the battlements as Duncan arrives. Suggest what he might have said to his travelling companions if he had been able to see her. How would this dialogue affect what Duncan says when he first meets her?

The Crown Sent Spinning

The symbolism of flags, language patterns, and costume helps us, as viewers, to read the images we are seeing without the need for dialogue. As a result, film can create meaning without words. The picture may not be worth a thousand words but it tends to reduce the need for words to a minimum. It may even create the possibility for words which could not be used without the images—as with Cawdor's final cry.

When Duncan is killed, his crown is knocked to the floor. The camera sees it spinning across the room. Orderly rule in the kingdom has been destroyed. When Lady Macbeth tells her husband "My hands are of your colour" and "A little water clears us of this deed," she suggests first that they can share the burden of their guilt but then that it is easily washed away and forgotten. Perhaps she foresees her future in the bloodied water we see in the

Establishing Shot 3

Reference to Pontius Pilate washing his hands of responsibility for the trial of Christ is a useful intertextual connection in helping to understand the symbolic gesture.

barrel but cannot accept it. Polanski never allows us to see her so clearly as at this point.

The symbolism associated with Macbeth's crowning as King of Scotland while standing on the Stone of Scone remains powerful today. The Stone of Scone is placed under the throne in Westminster Abbey when a king or queen of England, Scotland, Ireland, and Wales is crowned.

Meaning without Words

The opening and closing scenes from Polanski's *Macbeth* were added to the play-text by the screenwriters. Neither appears in the play-text and yet they each help to shape an interpretation which is not possible from the play-text.

The opening sequence which flows from the fog and returns to the fog suggests that what has happened can keep happening with every tide.

The closing sequence, in which Donalbain is about to visit the same witches' cave where Macbeth hallucinated the events of the play, suggests a return of these events. Just as the tide can reveal the events again and again, Polanski and Tynan suggest that the return is already taking place. The casting of Donalbain as a physical cripple may be suggesting that Macbeth is an emotional cripple, and therefore vulnerable to his wife's twisted ambitions. He is certainly excused from the banquet where he sees Banquo's ghost at the table on the basis of a recognized illness—probably epilepsy (from which Julius Caesar also suffered).

Cutaway 2 Take 7

Elizabethan attitudes to a number of common diseases and medical conditions are reflected in Shakespeare's works. Research the common attitudes to epilepsy in Elizabethan times. Use your findings to suggest how the audience might have responded to Macbeth's vision of Banquo's ghost. Compare this understanding with your own reaction to the appearance of the ghost.

Macbeth sees Banquo as he was murdered but the murderers have not told him what they did. Discuss how this knowledge affects your understanding of the way film is constructed to satisfy your needs as a viewer rather than to portray an accurate image of the events they seem to describe.

Ross and the Minor Characters

Although both Welles and Polanski retain most of the minor characters from *Macbeth*, these characters have little to say and tend to act as a chorus which allows us to see how the people around the events are seeing them. To maintain close interest in the storyline, the screenwriter tends to focus attention on the major characters. This focus usually leads to a reduction in the number of speaking parts in a film translation.

Polanski extends the role of Ross, however. Ross appears in every important scene. He does not always speak but he always sees what is happening. He takes the chain of office of Cawdor to Macbeth in the beginning to start the tragedy. He allows the assassins into Macduff's castle and confronts Lady Macduff before she is murdered. He then takes the news of their death to Macduff and Siward in England where they are waiting to overthrow Macbeth and return Malcolm to the throne. He becomes a surviving character who has no loyalty, who never seeks to rule but always has power because he is always on the winning side. Shakespeare's plays often feature characters who play small roles in the main storyline but who are successful in retaining their influence at court as rulers change. Casca fulfils a similar role in *Iulius Caesar*. As screenwriters, Polanski and Tynan have created Ross as a "political survivor" and reduced the number of speaking parts in a single action.

Cutaway 2 Take 8

The camera angles and lighting are useful pointers to the roles played by Ross at different points in the Polanski translation. Identify three important scenes in which Ross is a silent witness and compare the way he is lit and the angle he is filmed from in each sequence. Use these findings to suggest how Ross becomes one of the major characters in the screenplay without ever taking a major part in the action.

Consider how the role of Ross in Polanski's film establishes the power of the director to construct interpretations of events without changing the play-text.

Explore possible reasons for Polanski causing Ross's helmet to be knocked off during the final fight between Macduff and Macbeth. What does it suggest about Ross's future?

Further Opportunities for Discussion

1. Many of the famous sayings from Shakespearean plays can be found in *Macbeth* but not all of them are accurately used. Identify as many recognizable quotations as you can from the play-text and compare them with the way they are normally used. For example, "Lead on Macduff" is actually "Lay on Macduff." What others can you find?

2. One of the weakest scenes in the Polanski translation contains one of the most famous quotes from the play, "Is this a dagger I see before me? . . ." How would you change the filming of the scene to strengthen it?

3. Many of Shakespeare's play-texts contain a philosophical speech suggesting the importance of the events being played on the stage. Often these speeches refer to the stage itself. "All the world's a stage . . ." is one example. In *Macbeth*, the play-text includes the lines, "Life's but a walking shadow. . . . It is a tale/Told by an idiot, full of sound and fury,/Signifying nothing." Suggest how the inclusion of this speech supports the addition of the opening and closing scenes in the Polanski film.

4. Films exert control over the viewers' opportunities to interpret what the director has constructed. Referring to specific shots, describe how, through distance and angle, the camera marks the rise and fall of Macbeth from the opening sequences in the story to the close.

Director's Cut 1 The recent film translation of Shakespeare's early revenge tragedy, *Titus Andronicus*, provides a glimpse of the similarities between Elizabethan times and our own. A demand for revenge that leads to further demands for revenge must end in total destruction. The only light in this translation of Titus is the slow walk into the dawn by Titus Andronicus's grandson at the close of the film. There are no lines to support the interpretation but it does suggest the potential for union between black and white—a union totally rejected by the Moorish father of the bastard child of the conquered queen. Consider the view that tragedy can only work in a drama if there is a lighter and more balanced social context within which it occurs and against which it is compared.

The film translation of *Titus* suggests some of the themes that will later be developed in Shakespeare's more mature works. Most obvious is Macduff's revenge on Macbeth for the slaughter of his wife and family. This revenge restores the throne to its rightful heir. Consider how the execution of the Thane of Cawdor and the death of Macbeth can be seen as an opening and a closing for Shakespeare's exploration of ambition as sufficient motivation for treason.

CHAPTER THREE

Henry V

Establishing Shot 1

Film has frequently been used to promote a specific political view and its place as an entertainment allows it to be used to suggest that careful thought is unnecessary while viewing. Laurence Olivier's *Henry V* was created as a propaganda entertainment for the British facing defeat during World War II. Branagh's translation reflects an anti-war reaction to British involvement in the Falkland Islands of the South Atlantic. Because the two major film translations have been developed for opposing purposes, they provide rich opportunities for considering the original playwright's intentions.

The opening credits of the 1944 translation of *Henry V* directed by Laurence Olivier dedicate the film "To the Commandoes and Air borne Troops of Great Britain. The spirit of whose ancestors it has been humbly attempted to capture in some scenes." An apparently blank page flutters from a cloudless sky. At rest, it is revealed as a poster:

The Chronicle History
Of
King Henry the FIFT
With his battell fought
At Agincourt
In France
BY
Will Shakespeare
Will be played by
The Lord Chamberlain's Men
AT THE
GLOBE PLAYHOUSE
THIS DAY
The First of May 1600

The poster fades to a long shot of a white castle across the River Thames. A theatre appears in the bottom left of the screen, set in idyllic grounds with sculpted lawns and clear blue waters behind. The camera pans to a second theatre. Its flag, which says "The Globe Theatre," is raised. A trumpet calls theatre patrons. The orchestra plays as patrons enter. Some gentlemen prance foppishly about the stage. A page enters with a placard announcing the play. He gives way to the Chorus.

The artificial cleanliness, order, and tranquility of Olivier's setting represents a romanticized seventeenth century far removed from the crowded, dark, and unsewered reality. The splendour of the setting supports a necessary view—Britain will triumph at Agincourt. Olivier's opening to *Henry V* foregrounds the flamboyant pageantry of the film and promotes a vision of victory far removed from the demoralizing night bombing of London, the devastation of Coventry Cathedral, and the sorry retreat from Dunkirk.

Establishing Shot 1

Each translation must be read in the context of the time and place the film was made if we are to decide whether our reading is being "fair" to the film. We cannot expect a film to be read against the historical, cultural, and social context it was made in.

Cutaway 3 Take 1

Olivier's aerial opening shot of London shows the infamous tower, London Bridge with its multi-level housing, and the location of the theatres across the sparkling river from London town. As audience, we see London from the outside. We become part of the theatre crowd and not the actors. As a result, we are outsiders to both London life and to the events that will unfold on stage. Suggest how Olivier's translation supports a view that the war is outside the lives of the common people.

How does Olivier allow his audience to see Henry's war as an entertainment and their own war as an event beyond their control?

Use your responses to these questions to discuss ways in which Olivier's film might have provided comfort for an audience weary of being bombed as they faced repeated news of defeats and retreats such as Dunkirk.

Post-Falklands Britain, 1989

In harsh contrast to Olivier's idealized vision of "London as paradise," Kenneth Branagh's 1989 translation of *Henry V* to screen followed Britain's 1982 war with Argentina in the South Falkland Islands over an apparently non-strategic territory, which some called "a remnant of empire."

Branagh's opening plunges the viewer into darkness punctuated by ten seconds of shrill and ominous music. The darkness is broken by a series of credits in small red lettering against a black background. It climaxes with the title:

Henry V

The music takes on a deeply resonating tone and the contrasting melodies combine as Kenneth Branagh's name appears on screen. Casting and artistic credits continue against a musical score that evokes a death march. Again the screen fades to silence and darkness. At this point the screen has been dark for almost two minutes.

Cutaway 3 Take 2

A voice in the dark heightens our sense of anticipation. A match flares and we see a face. Consider the expectations you have experienced to this point. Are they supported by the words spoken by the Chorus?

If you can control the viewing, stop the film as the Chorus announces

"... the Play." Working in small groups, brainstorm and make note of the words you can recall from listening to the Prologue. Who are the principal characters? Where will the action take place? What are the major issues? What do these words suggest the story will be about? Use these notes as predictions during your first viewing of Branagh's film.

Suggest how the selection and emphasis of particular words can provide information about the play without our following every sentence in detail. What does this suggest about the construction of important speeches in Shakespeare's play-text?

Consider the impact of changing from match-flame to general stage lighting. How does this affect your expectations?

Consider the navy blue overcoat and black scarf of the Chorus. What links do his beard and costume suggest for you? Suggest ways in which Branagh may be making conscious links with Olivier's production.

Director's Cut 1 Both Branagh and Olivier provide the full Prologue to their translation of the play-text. From your study of the Prologue as it is presented on film, suggest why each director might see this speech as important to the opening of their production.

Branagh's Chorus, Derek Jacobi, is a famous Shakespearean stage actor as well as an experienced film actor. Discuss the advantages and disadvantages of this mix of experience in his presentation of Chorus.

Branagh was filming in 1988 when the popularity of both the royal family and the government of Margaret Thatcher were declining. In this context, Branagh offers a more three-dimensional King Henry, complete with character flaws and ambiguities. His inclusion of Henry's less noble deeds appears to provide greater depth and realism to the translation. The use of flashbacks reveals Henry's conscience and inner turmoil while providing the historical context and relationships established for the original Shakespearean audience in *Henry IV*, parts 1 and 2 (see Chronology).

Director's Cut 1 Research the careers of the better-known Elizabethan playwrights. List authors who spent time in jail for their play-writing and identify what laws they broke in their plays.

Olivier manipulates the play-text by omitting certain scenes in order to construct a particular reality for the audience of the time. Branagh's translation is equally constructed. The silhouetted movement of three vaguely comical figures along the skyline (they might be Monty Python's "Goodies") sig-

Establishing Shot 2

Writing about British and French royalty was always dangerous ground for playwrights in Elizabethan times. By law, they could only perform under licence and every play had to be granted permission by the Lord Chamberlain. Playwrights were liable to imprisonment or execution if they were thought to be presenting treasonous materials. This law remained in force in Britain until 1968.

Establishing Shot 3

Public performance was banned in England because of the high level of criminal activity that usually surrounded companies of performers. Members of crowded audiences were easy targets for pickpockets and cutpurses, while burglary was simple because people left their homes to watch the performance.

nals the shift from the palace interior of the early scenes to the English coast before the departure for France. Like a television news announcer present at the actual event, a greatcoat-clad Chorus stands before the legendary white cliffs of Dover. He speaks into the rising wind and music to announce the change of location and summarize the action.

Cutaway 3 Take 3

Select one of the scenes omitted from the Olivier film listed below and read the play-text scene from which it is deleted.

- the conspiracy of the Archibishop of Canterbury with the Bishop of Ely (I, i)
- the aristocratic conspirators (II, ii)
- Henry's blood-curdling threats before Harfleur (III, iii)
- the hanging of Bardolph (III, vi)
- Henry's attempt to bargain with God in the latter part of the "Upon the King" soliloquy (IV, i)

Consider the effect of the scene as played in Branagh's translation. Discuss the effect of deleting it. Suggest ways in which Olivier's omissions contribute to the concept of Henry as a noble and fearless leader.

How does Olivier's decision to omit these scenes provide a different bias in interpreting the dispute between France and England that leads to the Battle of Agincourt?

Branagh's camera cuts to the interior of a building in Southampton. Three dukes are revealed as traitors after arguing that traitors should be denied mercy when they are punished for treason. Despite his fury at being betrayed by his close friends and confidantes, this scene provides a contrasting image to the introduction of Henry as younger and much smaller than the members of his parliament. The inexperienced Henry receives the tennis balls as an insult from France; this Henry is both clever and ruthless.

Cutaway 3 Take 4

Cambridge, Grey, and Scroop are portrayed as youthful and inexperienced in Branagh's production. Their loyalty has been bought with French money. Consider how Branagh's camera angles and his grouping of the traitors shows their apparent youth and inexperience. Do they condemn themselves out of their own mouths when they deny mercy for the man whom Henry suggests may have spoken too much because he was drunk?

Suggest how the inclusion of this scene in Branagh's translation of the play-text provides a link between the tennis balls insult of Louis, the Dauphin, and Henry's war against the French.

Comedy and the Commoners

Olivier represents Nym, Bardolph, Pistol, and Mistess Nell Quickly as comic characters. Branagh portrays them with greater realism, as representatives of the common people who become the frontline troops in battle, who suffer at war, and who wait at home for news. In Branagh's translation of the play-text, their discussions provide insight into the thoughts of the commoners at each essential point in the development of the storyline.

By including fragments from the earlier *Henry IV*, Part 1, Branagh builds an image of Sir John Falstaff, childhood friend and advisor to Henry. The scene provides an insight into the relation between king and commoners which later informs the hanging of Bardolph. After Harfleur, the commoners provide a response to Henry's decree against chevauchée. Before Agincourt, they provide a reflection of opinion on the king's actions.

Olivier's comic commoners, in contrast, entertain the audience after complex discussion and before dire events, often showing disrespect to their superiors. Yet they are submissive to orders, and their suffering as they advance is emphasized; Olivier's Henry is clearly conscious of his responsibility to maintain their morale.

Branagh's commoners are more common. They grumble, brawl among themselves and express conflicting views of loyalty to their king and country. By comparing Branagh's commoners to Olivier's, the jingoistic intention of Olivier's screen translation becomes obvious. No population is as uniformly loyal, patriotic, steady in its purpose, or uniform in its view of events as Olivier's Britons at war. The crimes of war that result in Bardolph's execution are omitted from Olivier's film. Lack of resolve before Harfleur is treated as petty malingering and comically treated with a whack about the buttocks with the flat of a well-intentioned broadsword. The contrast between Branagh's and Olivier's commoners suggests that Olivier needs an entry point into the essential spirit of the British while Branagh may be seeking to display a more knowing and long-suffering society.

The most intriguing comic action in Olivier's film occurs between the two bishops. Olivier presents the bishops as a pair of clowns with the Australian ballet dancer and actor Robert Helpmann playing the Bishop of Ely. The Marx Brothers' slapstick-style comedy represented the popular vaude-

 Key Shot Chevauchée refers to a wartime expedition that aims to destroy as many villages and cause as much destruction and grief as possible. Churches were particularly targeted.

ville culture of the 1930s and 1940s. Thus, the resemblance of the Bishop of Ely's hair to that of Harpo Marx would have been as readily identifiable to a mid-twentieth century audience as is the trademark "Doh!" of Homer Simpson to a contemporary audience.

Cutaway 3 Take 5

Comedy is often built on the discomfort and incapacity of people who are otherwise competent. Gather examples of this approach to comedy from Shakespearean plays and from popular television sources. How does Olivier use these to develop comedy in *Henry V*?

Compare Olivier's and Branagh's direction of the dialogue between the two bishops. How does each create a motivation for war? On what grounds would you consider going to war as a soldier for either of the film Henry's?

Katharine is portrayed as a comic figure in her attempt to learn English. How are the feelings of women used to create comedy in such heavily male-oriented film translations?

Social Construction of the Film Translation

Every text is a product of its social and historical context. Olivier's film was commissioned by the government during war-time for the purpose of raising morale among the British population. As a result, it is focussed on the chivalry and heroism of battle. Suggestions of treason and murder are played down or completely omitted.

Branagh's text, following the brutality and apparent meaninglessness of the Falklands' campaign provides a more detailed account of the atrocities of war. In the wake of films such as *Platoon* and *Apocalypse Now*, Branagh's battle scenes are muddy, bloody melees relying on close-ups, slow motion, and an assault on the audience by sight and sound.

Cutaway 3 Take 6

Consider the influence of films such as *Pulp Fiction* (1994), dir. Quentin Tarantino; *Braveheart* (1995), dir. Mel Gibson; *Seven* (1995), dir. David Fincher; and *Scream* (1996), dir. Wes Craven on our response to the violence of Branagh's *Henry V*.

Even though Branagh's translation is relatively recent, we view it with a further twelve years of cinematic and media experience. We can draw on the media treatment of the Gulf War of 1991, the United Nations bombing of Yugoslavia, and the more recent Arab/Israeli conflicts. We have seen TV series such as *JAG* and *West Wing*, and films like *Top Gun* and *Men of Respect*. This experience allows us to make clear comparisons of the treatment of war as successful political action and as public relations disaster.

Standing before the breach his troops have made in the city walls, Branagh's Henry on a rearing white horse provides a symbol of the legendary heroism of St. George killing the dragon. At the same time, it establishes the very real danger of trying to storm through the gap. It is not surprising that his men are afraid. It is much more surprising to find the news reporter, Chorus, so close to the action—and where is the newsreel cameraperson? The play-text locates the action less dramatically, although many of Shakespeare's audience may have had direct experience of such action. And we should remember that the stage directions have been added later.

> *During the siege. Noises of battle (alarm). Enter King Henry, Exeter, Bedford, Gloucester, and soldiers with scaling ladders. (III, i)*

Comparison of the two film versions of the battle for Harfleur suggests two different approaches to war reporting and Branagh's physical size as the warrior-king supports his depiction as the underdog. Against enormous odds, Branagh's Henry triumphs by inspiration and personal charisma, Olivier's Henry by his goodness and the rightness of his cause.

Cutaway 3 Take 7

Consider the effect of Olivier's setting the Harfleur scene on the shores of France before any conflict begins. How does this influence the sense of urgency of the scene?

Compare the fresh appearance of Olivier's soldiers with Branagh's. How does this difference affect your interpretation of the scene?

Working in small groups, consider different ways of presenting the "Once more unto the breach . . ." speech. Perform the speech with the audience responding differently each time, for example, cheering during the speech, cheering only at the end, muttering rebelliously, glaring in silence. As a whole group, discuss the dominant feeling evoked by each performance.

Chevauchée

In Branagh's translation of the play-text to screen, Henry's brutal threat of chevauchée is explicit at Harfleur:

. . . Take pity of your town and of your people,
whiles yet my soldiers are in command . . .
If not, why, in a moment look to see
the blind and bloody soldier with foul hand
defile the locks of your shrill-shrieking daughters
your fathers taken by their silver beards
and their most reverend heads dashed to the walls
your naked infants spitted upon pikes
while the mad mothers with their howls confused/do break the clouds . . .
What say you? Will you yield, and thus avoid?
Or guilty in defense and be thus destroyed? (III, iii)

Branagh's passionate delivery is chilling, possibly casting doubt on Henry's sanity at this point in the battle. But it is his first battle as king. He must succeed if he is to lead his troops, and his country.

In contrast, however, he is later seen to be strongly against unnecessary violence and disorder when he supports the execution of his commoner friend, Bardolph, and condemns his sacrilegious theft:

We would have all such offenders cut off, and we give express charge that in our marches through the country there be nothing compelled from the villages, nothing taken but paid for, none of the French upbraided or abused in disdainful language. For when lenity and cruelty pay for a kingdom, the gentler gamester is the soonest winner. (III, vi)

Cutaway 3 Take 8

Olivier cut both of these speeches from his translation although the second suggests a leader with a very strongly developed moral sense. Consider the possibilities provided by deleting Bardolph's theft while retaining the second speech. How could the speech be changed to retain its meaning?

Work in small groups to consider how the speech could be delivered and how it would be received by the troops. Outline the changes you suggest and present your interpretation for discussion by the whole group.

Justifications for War

Henry argues that he is "No King of England if not King of France." He bases his demand for the French realm on the Archbishop of Canterbury's interpretation of the Salic Laws and the successes of his ancestor Edward (1294) in capturing French territory lost by successive British kings over the next several hundred years. The play is not historically accurate and the extent to which the arguments are reasonable is a matter for historians to debate. Shakespeare's play-text uses them to provide a period of reflection on the evening before the decisive battle of Agincourt. By this point, Henry has rallied his battle-weary troops to capture Harfleur, wintered in Calais, and fought his way across France. Branagh shows this progression as a cold and rain-soaked endurance trial. Olivier's progress is mapped and seems more comfortable.

Cutaway 3 Take 9

Fluellen is approached by Pistol to plead for Bardolph's life after he steals from a church. Fluellen rejects his plea. Suggest why Olivier omitted this scene when it shows that the British army is under strong leadership.

Olivier and Branagh present their pre-dawn walk among the troops in similar ways but the backgrounds to their walk and the conditions in which the troops are camping suggest very different interpretations. What are the major differences between the two translations?

Henry's disguised visiting among the troops on the evening before the battle of Agincourt establishes him as a concerned and caring leader. It also establishes the regard in which he is held by most of his troops. Despite the fact that they are tired, sick, and battle-weary, Henry is able to play on their loyalty. He is a popular leader and both Olivier and Branagh play this scene to establish that quality. Each director focusses on the leadership qualities that ensure Henry's success but they provide different emphases to meet different audience needs.

The Attributes of Monarchs

The Arden edition of *Henry V*, edited by H. Walter (1992), lists the following leadership qualities and conditions optimal for an Elizabethan king or queen:

- devout Christian
- learned and well-versed in theology
- just, merciful, not personally vengeful
- self-controlled
- advised by wise counsellors
- familiar with humble people but uncorrupted by contact
- seeks to defend and preserve the state
- concerned with the affairs of state—which concern him/her

- seeks to eradicate bad elements (idlers, parasites, and flatterers)
- hates empty ceremony and flattery
- is married
- is concerned about the cost of war, its evils for his/her people

Cutaway 3 Take 10

Identify events and speeches which establish each of Henry's leadership qualities in each of the film translations. In view of the leadership qualities expected by an Elizabethan audience, assess the likelihood of success for both Olivier's Henry and Branagh's Henry as leader of the British army.

Chorus

 Key Shot Voice-over—narration or dialogue continues from one shot to the next.

Having introduced the play, Olivier's Chorus takes on an almost mystical presence, fading in and out of scenes, voicing over blackouts, and recalling us to our role as Shakespearean audience members if we get too involved in the story. It is the Chorus who takes us from the staged performance of *Henry V* to the "real" world of Henry at Southampton. Olivier's move from the confines of the Globe Theatre to the more expansive, though still stylized, world of Elizabethan England leaves the Chorus with a difficult task. He must inform us of the apparent reality developing in the story but he must also maintain us as audience to a Shakespearean play. The extent to which he can succeed is a matter of personal response for a contemporary audience.

Branagh's Chorus is a more specific character. A media commentator, he appears at points where the reporter can provide us with the latest news flash. He lives within range of the cannons and shares the discomfort of the British army. At Harfleur, Branagh places his Chorus among the troops. Sweating and ducking from the cannon-fire, this Chorus is very much involved with the action while reporting it to the audience as onlookers.

Cold and perhaps disillusioned, Branagh's Chorus comes to the feet of the hanged Bardolph. He tells of the misery of camp life and the preparation for tomorrow's battle. As night falls, he walks into the mist and fog of the British camp.

In the Olivier text, the Chorus makes a final appearance alone against a night sky. He then recedes and fades away as the action moves from the stage to the realm of "movie." Olivier employs the film technique of voice-overs to represent the Chorus throughout the remainder of the film.

Director's Cut 3

Some critics have argued that the true voice and thoughts of Shakespeare are spoken by the Chorus. Do you think that we are seeing Shakespeare's truthful voice through the Chorus in either the Olivier or the Branagh translation? Is it reasonable or even possible to present Shakespeare's truthful voice in a contemporary production?

Speech and Inspiration

The film *Army Intelligence* provides a modern translation of Henry's inspiration St. Crispin's Day speech. Set in an American military training camp, the speech is used to inspire a platoon of outcast army recruits. The storyline of the film is intended to establish the timeless quality of Shakespeare's language and its ability to inspire all people through all ages. Though the setting is hardly believable, the rain-soaked delivery of the speech offers a valuable contrast for both the Branagh and Olivier translations.

Mel Gibson's (1995) film *Braveheart* is historically closer to *Henry V* so it becomes possible to compare the films in terms of arms, costume, weapons, and military strategy. At a more basic level, it is interesting to compare the audience impact of the rallying speech before the final battle with the Olivier and Branagh battle speeches.

Although much of the focus of *Henry V* must be on the battle scenes, these are contrasted with more sympathetic scenes. The surrender of Harfleur under threat of chevauchée is followed with the comedy of Katharine's English lesson. The common touch presented through Nell Quickly, Nym, Pistol, and Bardolph establishes a social context for the troops who follow Henry and his noblemen into battle, who walk while their leaders ride, and who are prevented from profiting from the war when Henry declares the ban on chevauchée. The final scene of the play-text establishes that Henry is a humble man, eager to marry, one who seeks the best for his state and for his people—the perfect leader for the Elizabethan audience.

Director's Cut 4

Queen Elizabeth's unmarried status provided a powerful potential for political alliances. Research the period of Elizabeth's long reign to establish those alliances formed on the basis of potential marriage. Use the findings from your research to suggest Shakespeare's opinion of political alliances through engagement or marriage.

Romance and the Portrayal of Women

In her recent novel, *Lady Dance,* set in the plague period of 1347–1349, Australian author Jackie French notes that a woman might have twenty babies but only two or three were likely to survive. More than two hundred years after this plague, Shakespeare's Juliet (in *Romeo and Juliet*) is only thirteen when she marries Romeo. Her father asks Paris to wait until she is at least fifteen before she is married because she is his only surviving child. Marriage among the nobility in Shakespeare's times was arranged for the benefit of the parents, not the lovers, and this approach is still common in some places—though the age for the marriage has tended to rise among those who can afford to keep their daughters at home for longer than their poorer neighbours.

In *Henry V,* the only age references inform us that Henry is young. The bishops discuss his wild youth but accept his deep learning. As a result, it is difficult to determine his actual age—even though the French king insults him with the gift of tennis balls and its implication that Henry is only fit to play a child's game. Even less information is available about the age of the French princess, Katharine. Film directors cast according to cost and availability of actors. Zeffirelli broke with the tradition of casting experienced actors in difficult roles to cast unknown children as Romeo and Juliet in his film translation of that play. The choice created a whole new interpretation of the play but its motivation had substantial financial benefits.

Branagh's casting of his wife of the time, Emma Thompson, as Katharine allowed for a contemporary match with his casting as Henry, though it had no necessary advantage in interpreting the role. For an Elizabethan king, Katharine may, just as easily, have been thirteen. In fact, played by a boy, this would have been a simpler age to match appearance with.

Cutaway 3 Take 11

Consider the possibility of casting Olivier's Katharine into Branagh's film. How would this affect the relationship between Henry and Katharine? What changes would need to be made in the final surrender scene? If you were able to cast Nicole Kidman as Katharine, who would you cast as Henry? Provide a set of notes to support your decision for the producers. How important is the casting of Katharine to your enjoyment of each film?

While the sub-plot leading to Henry's marriage is relatively unimportant for both Olivier and Branagh, neither rejects it completely. Discuss the dramatic importance of the introduction of Katharine in the English lesson. How is Katharine's role developed as Henry woos her with a mix of English and French? How important is it to your understanding of Katharine's role that her marriage to Henry is the first of the terms of French surrender?

Director's Cut 5

Despite the fact that Henry has brutally devastated her father's kingdom and disinherited her brother, Katharine seems excited about the impending marriage. From your research of the Elizabethan period, consider Katharine's possible future if Henry had not defeated the French. Using the discussions between Katharine and Alice during the English lesson, consider Katharine's likely knowledge of Henry.

Though English had replaced French as the official language at England's court, Henry would have spoken fluent French. In addition, noblewomen were married to noblemen by arrangement so Henry's wooing is unnecessary. To what extent does the comical interpretation allow contemporary audiences to argue that Shakespeare's play-texts are "eternally relevant"?

Olivier provides interesting insights into the relationship between Queen Isabel and the French king during the surrender scene. At another interpretive extreme, Branagh completely omits the role of Isabel. Instead, he provides Henry with her final speech. This changes the power relationships and suggests alternative readings of the play-text.

Cutaway 3 Take 12

Draw pictures showing the relationships of the major characters in the surrender scene as they appear in each of Olivier's and Branagh's translations. Consider the levels, heights, and distance from the camera of each of the key characters. Suggest how the positioning of characters within a single shot allows the director to establish the power relationships between them.

To what extent do the director's uses of light and colour influence the composition of the shots?

Discuss the use of camera angles to foreground the importance of some individuals while diminishing others.

Further Opportunities for Discussion

1. After you have re-read the Prologue to the play-text of *Henry V*, re-view both the Olivier and Branagh texts on screen. Working in small groups,

discuss the similarities and differences between the two Choruses in terms of setting, costume, function, and fairness to script. Discuss the effectiveness of each chorus in using the Prologue to establish a clear vision of the direction in which the entertainment will develop.

2. The placard used to introduce the play in Olivier's translation was not a feature of Elizabethan theatre. In fact, most of the audience were unlikely to have been literate. Placards would, however, have been quite familiar to the war-time English audience because they were commonly use to introduce acts or "turns" in vaudeville theatre still common in Olivier's period. Consider the role of the placards in your own understanding of the Prologue in Olivier's translation to film. Consider how placards might suggest entertainment for the originally intended audience in British theatres during war-time.

3. At the time of Shakespeare's production, French had recently been replaced by English as the official court language. In portraying the French royalty as welcoming the imposition of English, Shakespeare may have been capturing the rising feelings of nationalism and patriotism associated with the English language. As a result, this scene could have been uproariously funny to the Elizabethan audience. To what extent should Olivier be able to harness similar feelings among his intended war-time British audience?

4. *Henry V* was probably written between *Henry IV*, parts 1 and 2 and *Hamlet* (see Chronology). Some critics have argued that the relative absence of Falstaff is symptomatic of the move away from comedy towards the epic and historical. It is also apparently true that the actor who created Falstaff was no longer with the company. Consider the extent to which we interpret plays on the basis of our own knowledge.

5. Most directors create productions which position their audience into interpreting what is seen according to the director's wishes rather than their own. Find examples of films or play productions where you have been unconvinced by the director's interpretation. Use these examples to discuss ways in which directors can manipulate audiences and contrast these with examples where the director fails. What are the elements for effective direction to meet audience needs?

6. Branagh's Henry bluffs the surrender of Harfleur by threatening its mayor with terrible destruction. Olivier omits the speech completely. Is it reasonable to omit entire speeches from a Shakespearean interpretation? Suggest a set of rules for fair treatment when directing a Shakespearean play production.

Narration

Key Shot

The first element of narrative film-making is called narration. Narration is any device which helps to join parts of the story together logically to establish sequentiality.

"Once Upon A Time"

U nderstanding the way film is constructed is similar to under-standing the way a novel or a play is constructed. We can use similar words to describe what is happening.

In most western countries influenced by American films, the construction of a film (including news and documentary programs) is based on four fundamental elements: narration, sequentiality, spatial relationships, and closure. These are the same elements we use when we write a narrative story.

A narrator is a storyteller whose role is often to introduce or join together events which do not happen immediately after each other or in the same place or at convenient time intervals. Like the newsreader who provides a commentary for images from an on-site broadcast, the narrator tells us how to "read," how to interpret, what we are seeing. In Greek theatre the role of the narrator was performed by the chorus and, in some of Shakespeare's play-texts, the narrator is titled Chorus (for example, in *Henry V*).

Some Shakespearean plays, such as *Troilus and Cressida,* begin with a spoken prologue which sets the scene. *Julius Caesar* opens with a group of townspeople who explain that the play opens on a public holiday. In *Othello,* Shakespeare uses Iago's wife, Emilia, to move between Desdemona, Iago, and Michael Cassio. In filming *Macbeth,* Polanski uses Ross to provide logical sequence as we move with a known character between unrelated scenes. Ross sees the murder of Banquo and of Lady Macduff but he also comes to the English camp and tells these events to Siward and Macduff.

Narration on film has the same purpose as literary narration. We are familiar with a number of narrative devices that are used to link scenes. Polanski uses fog to change from the opening scene with witches to the battlefield with the king, sunsets come before dawn, zooming towards a door or a window suggests that the next scene will be inside.

A more literary film device is the use of voice from one scene to carry over into the next or to describe one event while we watch another. Branagh uses this voice-over technique as he delivers the "Once more into the breach" speech in *Henry V* while we watch his soldiers' faces change from fear and defeat to bravery again. Often, however, the voice-over is performed by someone removed in time or place from a scene, or as a lead-in to it.

The camera only allows us to see characters and events as the filmmaker wants them to be seen. The camera angle provides another key element in

 Zoom—the camera lens is adjusted to make the subject appear to move towards (zoom in) or away (zoom out) from the camera.

the grammar we need to read film. In more familiar terms, it focusses us on a single point of view. We are used to looking up to heroes and looking down on people who are weak or threatened. Looking down with a down shot can be used to show us people in danger.

A long shot with a telephoto lens across a room full of people can tell us that someone is in love with the character at the other end of the long shot. Lucentio falls in love with Bianca at first sight from a distance in Zeffirelli's *Taming of the Shrew*. Tybalt glimpses the hated Romeo across a room full of partying people in Luhrmann's *Romeo and Juliet*. The long shot of Lady Macbeth combing her hair at her dressing table prevents us from coming close enough to understand her state of mind. Her apparent isolation may suggest her detachment from human values or feeling. Polanski leaves the reading of the scene to us as readers and, in the process, opens options for interpretation which may not be available in other translations.

Key Shot Camera angle—the angle from which the camera is "looking at" the subject.

Key Shot Down shot—the camera is tilted to look down at the subject.

Establishing Shot 1
Power relationships are established on stage with voice, costume, and position. In film, they are also established by using camera angles to create a point of view.

Director's Cut 1
In the balcony scene in the play-text of *Romeo and Juliet*, Juliet is at home in her room upstairs while Romeo is outside on ground level. In Baz Luhrmann's film, the director brings Romeo into the garden and then brings Juliet outside to join him. Discuss how the power relationship between the two lovers is established by the director's decision to bring Juliet into the garden on the same level as Romeo instead of having her on the balcony with Romeo needing to climb up from below.

Music plays an important part in most films. It is used to establish historical time, to set mood, and to create suspense. It may also be used to show the connection between characters or events. Polanski uses a range of music from rock to unaccompanied boy soprano in *Macbeth* while Zeffirelli uses classical orchestral and solo instrumental music in *Hamlet*. The type of music used by filmmakers may suit the narrative but it must also suit the audience that the filmmaker has in mind when the film is made. Luhrmann's rock-and-rap score is appropriate to the young audience he has directed *Romeo and Juliet* towards; it is also very appropriate for establishing the period in which the film is set.

Speech (called dialogue in play-texts and film scripts) can be more powerful on film than in literature because there is no need for the vision to stop while we hear what is being said. We know why Mel Gibson is being mean (dialogue) to Ophelia in Zeffirelli's *Hamlet* because we can see (visual) that he knows Claudius and Polonius are spying on him.

Music, images, and camera angles can be used together with dialogue to provide information in ways which are not possible in books because of the need most of us have to read along lines one at a time. Even if we skim, the story can only be told in a single sequence.

"There's no art to find the mind's construction in the face" (I, iv) says Duncan in *Macbeth*. But the film-maker's construction is equally difficult to see because the strength of film to demand that we use several senses at the same time makes the medium very powerful. This is one of the important reasons why we need to understand how film and television broadcasts are constructed—so that we can keep a critical or curious mind on the story and on how it is being told while we are "reading" the film. Our critical reading of a film must be able to match consciously the decisions the film-maker has made at every point in the film if we are to decide whether we agree with the interpretation. Reading critically does not mean that we set out to view the film so that we can criticize it in a negative way. Instead, it means that we watch and listen for the way the story is constructed at the same time as we watch and listen to enjoy the story.

Shakespeare's intention to provide entertainment was important. He had to be successful at the Elizabethan box office or his rival production companies would take his audience and he would lose money. The film-maker of the late twentieth century has the same problem. Films that cost $135 million to make need to be very successful to return a profit at the box office. Most Shakespearean films have been modestly budgeted by comparison with the latest blockbusters. Not many people would take the financial risk of translating a Shakespearean play into film unless the filmmaker and the stars were well known and popular. Hugh Heffner's decision to finance Roman Polanski's film production of *Macbeth* is a notable exception.

Editing is another way that films are narrated—some people call this cutting or they use the French word *montage*.

A film may be shown to us at the theatre or on the television screen as if the events happened one after the other in order. The reality is much more complicated.

Because films are not filmed in their final order and because actors sometimes make mistakes and because some shots have to be filmed or shot again and again, the editor is a most important person in deciding what the finished film will look like.

When the director decides to edit the film, the result is called a "director's cut." The director's cut is the final product the director has decided on. We would normally expect this to be the film we see in theatres or on television. Some films, however, are further cut to meet the demands of censors, to meet producer's demands, or to fit television screening schedules. When this happens we may never see the film the director intended us to see. At other times, the director might deliberately make the film to allow for different cuts. Kenneth Branagh made the film version of *Hamlet* to include the full four hours of the play-text though it was unlikely that the full film would be shown frequently or even widely in its complete form.

 Director's Cut 2   The second cut of Kenneth Branagh's four-hour film of the play-text of *Hamlet* is less than two hours long. It is worth comparing the two films to examine what Branagh chose as the most important part of the published text.

If a sequence is supposed to be very exciting—like the battle scenes from *Henry V* or the murder scene from *Julius Caesar*—the editor must cut the shots together to help create this effect. Very short shots from different camera angles help to create a fast, exciting effect while long shots with little action might help to make the scene more tense. The car chase sequence from *Bullitt* is an interesting example of short cutting to create fast-paced excitement.

Each of the following is an interesting example of editing for different moods and different audiences:

- the slaughter of Lady Macduff and her children in Polanski's *Macbeth*;
- the St. Crispin's Day speech from *Henry V* (IV, iii) by Olivier as compared with Branagh's treatment;
- Desdemona's speech to her father about the responsibilities of a daughter from Parker's *Othello* and Capulet's advice to Paris in Zeffirelli's *Romeo and Juliet*.

Each is worthy of close examination to decide how the editor has assisted the film-maker in establishing a particular view of how the event is important in establishing a translation of the director's vision.

CHAPTER FIVE

Julius Caesar

Openings

Since the film-maker can presume that the cinema audience has already agreed to travel to the theatre and pay to see the film (it is a captive audience), the opening is probably not as important as it would be for a television film—where viewers can switch to another channel if their interest is not captured immediately.

Unlike the television film-maker, the theatrical film-maker has an opportunity to set up the play without fear that the audience will "change channels" from a play that looks boring from its opening scenes.

Cutaway 5 Take 1

View the openings of both the Burge and the Mankiewicz films. Working in script review groups of no more than four people, suggest some of the ways that the opening of the Mankiewicz or the Burge film would need to be altered to capture a television audience in the first few minutes of the production—before the first commercial break—and keep the audience from changing channels.

Historical Setting

Both film translations deviate from the Shakespearean play-texts by opening with quotations from Plutarch. The Mankiewicz film presents the text in a heavy, bold script on the screen. The Burge translation delivers the same text as a voice-over. Consider the reasons that both film directors felt it necessary to provide this historical background but that Shakespeare did not. What would be lost to you as a twenty-first century film reader if these historical notes were omitted from each film?

Opening Scenes

The Burge translation opens with a large bird circling the sky, caterwauling. The camera follows the bird—which turns out to be a vulture—as it settles on an overgrown battle field. An authoritative sounding male voice in funereal tones describes the battle which took place at the site. The relationship

Establishing Shot

At least 42 different versions of *Julius Caesar* have been made for film or television presentation. This chapter focusses on the two best-known film versions:
- directed by Joseph Mankiewicz (1953) starring Marlon Brando
- directed by Stuart Burge (1969) starring Charlton Heston

between the vulture and the Roman Imperial eagle remains unstated but we may begin to make some associations.

Film Credits

The Mankiewicz film presents the film credits as a list in heavy, bold lettering over the background of a stylized cast metal eagle, the eagle of Imperial Rome, but the Burge translation uses the backdrop of a triumphal procession through the streets of Rome, flashing the actors' names and roles on the screen rather than including them in a continuous list.

Cutaway 5 Take 2

A continuous listing suggests continuities that may not exist in the reading being presented. The flashing of single-name credits suggests an isolation of characters from one another that may be equally misleading. How do the title sequences of each film translation relate the major players in your reading?

Consider the symbolism created by the juxtaposition of the skull and the chanting voices. What does this suggest about the way we should read the film?

Both the Mankiewicz and Burge films give top billing to Marc Antony (Marlon Brando in the former and Charlton Heston in the latter) listing Brutus (James Mason and Jason Robards respectively) second. Cassius is given third billing in the Mankiewicz film and Caesar in the Burge film, both characters played by John Gielgud.

Cutaway 5 Take 3

In Shakespeare's published play-texts, the "Dramatis Personae" begins by listing Caesar and his family and supporters. The Caesar group is followed by Brutus and his family and supporters, including the conspirators. Consider the ways in which this order of presentation constructs a translation of the play for the Elizabethan stage which is different from the film credits.

Explore significance in the order of presentation of the casting in each of the films. Is this Antony's play? Brutus's play? Caesar's play?

Music

Music can be used to create atmosphere or to suggest setting. Shakespeare was an Elizabethan Englishman writing a play which he set in Roman times in Italy. The Hollywood approach to music, until the seventies at least, has been to provide grand orchestral accompaniment to apparently historical films including large crowd scenes. Many films have one or several musical themes or signatures (for example, Zeffirelli's *Romeo and Juliet*). Some films are best remembered for a single piece of music (such as the themes from *Shaft* or *The Good, the Bad and the Ugly*).

More recent film music tends to use fewer instruments and more modern music and to integrate electronic sound effects into the musical score. The result is increasingly intended to create a sound track that stands alone as a commercial music product (for example, the sound track from *Titanic*). The expense of film-making suggests that this secondary merchandising can help cover initial production costs so that box office takings can be seen as profit for shareholders financing the film.

Cutaway 5 Take 4

Discuss the most obvious differences in the use of music between the two films.

Contrast the music used during the screen credits of the Mankiewicz and the Burge translations. Which instruments are featured? Describe the beat of each. Does either seem to you to be "Roman" music? Which musical score sounds more Elizabethan? Which sounds more like a contemporary concert band?

Select several dramatic scenes from one of the films and explain how the selection of instruments and the approach to the scene assists or hinders the development of the dramatic moment which is the focus of the scene.

Use your research notes to discuss how each film uses the musical score to establish setting and to extend the dramatic effect during important scenes.

Endings

The Mankiewicz translation of the play ends on the battlefield, but the Burge translation ends in the evening following the battle with the two successful generals marching between two long lines of their soldiers to Octavius's tent where the body of Brutus lies.

Omissions

You have probably noticed that theatres schedule films in two-hour slots and you may be aware that both the Mankiewicz (121 minutes) and the Burge (117 minutes) translations of the play omit a good deal of Shakespeare's play-text. At 2,450 lines, *Julius Caesar* is one of Shakespeare's shorter plays (compare *Hamlet* at 3,762 lines or *Richard III* at 3,600). Yet, the longer plays and the shorter ones generally have close to the same running time in the theatre. One indication of what is missing from *Julius Caesar* is found by comparing the Mankiewicz and Burge films with the Wise translation, which is basically a film of the complete stage play running 180 minutes. Another is to compare the films with a published play-text.

The decision to add or cut from an established play-text is dictated, in part, by the advantages and disadvantages presented by translation to the film medium itself (whether in colour or black and white, silent or sound).

A more significant consideration is the film-maker's intention in producing the play-text as a film. To be a commercial success, the film translation must convert to theatre attendance, to box office success. To achieve this success, it must pass the first principle of any Shakespearean performance: it must be entertaining. The second principle of any film is that it should make sense; that is, it must have a coherent plot with credible characters involved in action which is sufficiently well explained for us, as film readers, to become involved with, and feel some sympathy for, the characters.

Director's Cut 1

Act I, ii is a long scene (322 lines) which reveals a good deal about Brutus and Cassius through their conversations. Burge omits a significant number of Brutus's lines (37-50; 63-65; 83-89; 162-67; 303-306) and an even larger number of Cassius's lines (54-58; 66-78; 90-92; 100-115; 153; 156-61; 179-81; 297-302; 308-320). Although some of these omissions are a dozen lines or more, most are small cuts of five lines or fewer, suggesting that the director cut the play carefully and judiciously. Are there aspects of Brutus's and Cassius's characters which are lost through cutting these lines? What might the audience learn about Brutus's ego or the relationship between Brutus and Cassius in these lines that helps to understand later developments in the play? What is gained by the omission of these lines?

Mankiewicz, on the other hand, cuts very few of these lines (48-50; 74-76; 83; 112-115; 133-34; 156-57; 215; 262-67; 299). Compare the Mankiewicz and Burge films (scene ii) for both the information the audience gains and the pace of the films. Do you find that the Mankiewicz film drags during any of the lines that Burge omits?

The principles of film translation create tension for some Shakespearean play-text scholars who are, occasionally, inclined to treat the text as more important, from a literary viewpoint, than its meaningful translation to a reading audience. In this view, the printed text, in an apparently original form, is seen as a piece of literature which is complete in itself. The role of the text as a script for action is not seen to be as important.

If the literary view is disregarded in favour of the view that Shakespeare was intended to be performed as an entertainment, the consideration of cutting or adding dialogue to establish a meaningful translation becomes a case for making decisions which will vary among individuals, across generations, and across cultures. The range of translations included in this book shows how individual the decisions can be. Choices may depend on the country of origin of the film, the choice of screenwriters, the reputation of the actors, the intention of the director, or even the opinion of the producers who are providing the money for the film. Most of these possibilities are explored with humour in the film *Shakespeare in Love.*

In the following activities, you are asked to compare cuts made to the published play-texts by Mankiewicz and by Burge and to comment on the consequences of omitting lines and scenes.

Act I, i: Mankiewicz cuts about one-third of the first scene and Burge cuts over half of it. Both omit lines 15 to 19, banter between the officers and the saucy cobbler, and both omit parts of Flavius's speeches (lines 56-60 and lines 68-71). Examine these lines to see what is lost by their omission. Drama frequently contains redundant parts to make certain that the audience gets the playwright's message. What decisions have been made by the film-makers that allow them to delete the lines omitted here, either because they are redundant, or because they alter the focus in some way?

In Act II, iv, both the Mankiewicz and the Burge translations omit the scene with Portia, her servant boy, and the Soothsayer completely. What information does this scene provide? What is lost or gained through the omission of this scene? Consider how the scene might contribute to the pacing of each film and then suggest why each director or screenwriter may have omitted it.

The Burge translation omits the Act III, i sequence where Antony's servant brings a message from Antony to the conspirators. The Mankiewicz translation keeps it word for word. What does this scene reveal about the judgments of Brutus, Antony, and Cassius? If you were directing a film translation of the play-text, would you include or omit this scene?

In Act IV, i, the triumvirate—Antony, Octavius, and Lepidus—displays its evil side by making a hit list of its perceived enemies who must die (including a nephew and a brother), by acknowledging that it intends to subvert Caesar's will, by Antony's disparagement of Lepidus, and by petty quarrels between Antony and Octavius.

The Burge translation omits lines 7-27 and 31-47, rearranging Octavius's final speech. Mankiewicz, on the other hand, retains all of the scene except for Antony's vitriolic comments about Lepidus (lines 31-40). Compare the audience's perception of Antony's character in the two productions. Which production retains more of the noble Antony who defended his late friend Caesar at the Forum? If you directed a film translation of the play-text, which picture of Antony would you wish to present?

Additions to the Text

Both Mankiewicz and Burge add to Shakespeare's script at the beginning of Act II, ii. Mankiewicz shows Calpurnia waking from a dream, crying "Help, ho, they murder Caesar" three times, lines which were reported by Caesar in the play-text. Burge, on the other hand, adds even more, presenting a montage of images and voice-overs, incorporating words and phrases from Caesar's report of Calpurnia's dream—presented later in the scene (lines 76-81)—and Artemidorus's written "schedule" at the beginning of Act II, iii.

 Key Shot Montage— From French, it literally means "cutting." In film, it refers to the editing together of a number of otherwise disconnected elements to create a meaningful, and often more powerful, whole.

Cutaway 5 Take 8

Examine Burge's dream scene in detail. Is it an effective sequence in the film? If you were directing the film, would you include Burge's scene, would you stick to the Shakespearean script, or would you try another approach?

The Assassination and the Funeral

Two of the most powerful scenes in the play are the assassination and funeral scenes. These are the engines which drive the play through its various conflicts to the final resolution. The assassination scene contains the most bloody and horrific slaying of the great general and foe of Pompey. The depiction of this scene on film requires careful consideration of choreography and camera angles. The funeral scene is the pivotal scene in that it concludes with Marc Antony achieving the upper hand over the conspirators. The scene focusses on two magnificent speeches by Brutus and Antony, speeches which are going to determine what happens in the remainder of the play.

The Assassination Scene

SOUNDTRACK   In the Mankiewicz translation, there is absolute silence except for dialogue during the assassination. This silence contrasts greatly with the cries of liberty after the assassination. In the Burge production, there is an interesting percussive track which adds somehow to the horror of the action. Furthermore the film records the sounds of the daggers entering and leaving Caesar's body.

Cutaway 5 Take 9

Consider the two approaches described above in relation to the complete translation they appear in. How important is the background sound in each of these films?

Key Shot Choreography refers to the movement of actors within a scene. All movement—including the speed and direction of the movement—is planned, or "choreographed" so the camera can follow exactly what is required.

CHOREOGRAPHY AND THE DEPICTION OF VIOLENCE   There is little blood in the Mankiewicz translation. After the other senators stab Caesar, he walks towards Brutus, who delivers the final blow, whereupon Caesar crumples to the floor of the Senate. In the Burge translation, Caesar receives some initial stab wounds, walks to Brutus, who delivers a blow, but then walks back to the other side of the set where he is set upon and stabbed many times (Plutarch claims that Caesar was stabbed some twenty-three times). Consider when each of these films was made. The 1953 translation, made shortly after World War II, was a period of economic prosperity and post-war relief from a significant conflict. Burge's 1969 translation followed the assassinations of John F. Kennedy and Martin Luther King.

Cutaway 5 Take 10

What does each of these translations say about the cultural sensibilities of the times in which they were filmed? Which is the more effective? Explore the ways in which your own cultural context assists you in making your decisions about the presentation of the assassination in each film.

The Funeral Orations

VOICE   That movie stars can frequently be recognized by their voices alone suggests the importance of the sound track in a film. Of course, the way that each player interprets a scene is reflected in his or her voice: tone, pacing, pauses, volume, pitch, timbre. One effective way of analyzing actors' verbal interpretations is to compare the ways that two more actors deliver the same scene.

Cutaway 5 Take 11

Listen to the voices of Marlon Brando and Charlton Heston in the funeral scene. Which voice do you find to be more appealing and persuasive? If you were a citizen of Rome, which Antony do you think you would be more likely to trust—based on voice alone? Upon what would you base your decision?

CAMERA TECHNIQUES   In both translations the speakers are shot from below, and the crowd—the Roman citizens—is often shot from above. This tends to create a sense that power rests with the speakers rather than their audience. In the Burge translation, the camera comes close to Heston when he is touching citizens during the first part of the speech. When he is presenting the will, however, he is shot from below and stands by the huge columns that symbolize Imperial Rome. Describe ways that these shots match Marc Antony's intention to persuade the Romans to his viewpoint.

Casting

Casting is a very serious consideration for producers of films based on Shakespearean works. Often London stage actors have been used to lend a feeling of authenticity to the film translations (Olivier, Gielgud, Stewart, Morden). This has frequently been unsuccessful since stage actors do not always feel comfortable with film and appear to present exaggerated performances rather than play the part more naturalistically. Sometimes, however, the casting has proved interesting, for example, with Billy Crystal's grave digger in Branagh's *Hamlet*. At other times it has been disastrous—for example, with Jack Lemmon in the same film.

The Mankiewicz and Burge productions are strongly cast and we see this particularly in the role of Marc Antony. As film readers, you may be unfamiliar with either of the actors who play this role; this can be an advantage in evaluating their acting since they are less likely to be prejudged on the basis of their names or fame.

Cutaway 5 Take 12

In your opinion, who appears to be more effective as Brutus, Jason Robards or James Mason?

Who is the more effective Portia?

Note the casting of the older Gielgud as Julius Caesar. Does Gielgud make a more or less effective Caesar than Louis Calhern?

If you were the casting director for a new translation of *Julius Caesar*, whom would you cast in the major roles? Write a justification of your decisions to satisfy your financial advisers.

Effects and Special Effects

Act I, iii opens with lightning and thunder which extend through Act II, ii. For special weather effects, Shakespeare made do with rolling a cannonball across the floor of the upper prop room and setting off a bit of gunpowder—which, as you probably know, led to the fire which burned down the original Globe Theatre in 1613—but film directors must create a more convincing show.

Gender Balance

Many of Shakespeare's play-texts suggest that the women are playing significant roles in support of the men who appear to be central (for example, Lady Macbeth). The roles of Portia and Calpurnia (sometimes spelled "Calphurnia") can be usefully explored from the point of view of the strength and dignity of women.

Views of the Critics

Film critics frequently make their reputations by writing acerbic, sarcastic observations about actors and productions which are both witty and perceptive. For example, here is Kenneth Rothwell describing Felix Aylmer's Brutus from the "Famous Scenes from Shakespeare, No. 1 (1945)" production:

An apprehensive ectomorph, this Brutus hardly seems capable of plotting the assassination of great Caesar. (Rothwell and Melzer, 114)

Of the same production, he notes

. . . the costumes look as though they had seen better days . . . but then again, I've rarely seen costumes for the Roman history plays that were very inspired. (Rothwell and Melzer, 115)

The comments are frequently quite cutting and one wonders how actors might respond to such comments as Tom Castner's on Jason Robards' Brutus:

Robards appears to be receiving his lines by concealed radio transmitter, and delivering them as part of the responsive reading in a Sunday sermon. (Rothwell and Melzer, 121)

Cutaway 5 Take 15

Speculate on Robards' private response to such trenchant criticism. View the movie and write a positive review of Robards' Brutus.

Locate a cutting movie review and write a review of the review.

McMurtry describes James Mason's Brutus as

deliberate, meditative, his eyes like great dark pools; he is convinced of his own nobility and thus convinces others. Meeting for the first time with the conspirators [II, i], he is calm and matter-of-fact rather than imperative, and step-by-step he takes the leadership away from Cassius, advising, among other things, that Marc Antony not be killed along with Caesar. The disastrous results of this and other of Brutus' advice seems to be noticed by nobody in the film, with the exception of the increasingly distressed Cassius. Sometimes, so great is Mason's hypnotic power, they are noticed by nobody in the audience either. (McMurtry, 1994, 87)

The role of the film critic in reviewing the director's achievement and the actor's performance seems to be acceptable. It is more difficult to see how the critic's opinion of the audience can assist us as film readers in understanding or appreciating the film. McMurtry's criticism of the audience, however, suggests that she expects film readers to be able to separate their personal involvement with the film from their critical reading of the film.

Cutaway 5 Take 16

Choose any major character, other than Brutus, from the film (for example, Caesar, Cassius, Marc Antony) and use McMurtry's review as a model to write your own interpretive review of the actor's suitability for the role.

Consider whether it is the role of the film critic to comment on audience response and suggest guidelines for such a commentary.

Camera Technique

The unusual profile shots of Brutus (James Mason) and Cassius (John Gielgud) in the Mankiewicz translation are similar to the images we can see on Roman coins of the period. Consider whether Mankiewicz and his cinematographer had a purpose for shooting in this manner. How do such camera angles add an intended atmosphere to the film? Would these shots have any bearing upon the casting?

Setting

The film translations of historical dramas, whether from the meta-narrative of the history books or from playwrights such as Shakespeare, have tended to be large screen epics featuring casts of thousands of extras overwhelming the screen with their sheer numbers. Often these films were filled with high tower shots panning great armies marching or refugees being driven from their homes. This tradition goes back to the earliest days of film-making. The advent of the wide screen and seventy millimetre film, however, literally widened the possibilities with epics such as *Ben Hur* and *Spartacus*.

Today the epic's technological offspring are generally special effects films such as *Titanic*. *Julius Caesar* contains many of the components which would render it a film epic. It has the grandeur of Imperial Rome and the battle scenes that were a part of almost all epic films. Look at the *Julius Caesar* productions in terms of scale. If the classic film epics included high, wide panoramic shots of thousands and lavish sets and costumes, how does *Julius Caesar* hold up against these types of films?

Examine a clip from a film such as *Ben Hur* or *Cleopatra* (which featured Elizabeth Taylor and Richard Burton many years before they starred in *The Taming of the Shrew*).

Consider the camera techniques used. How does the length of camera shot affect the epic aspect of the film? What kind of a perspective of Rome does the viewer get? Are the buildings shot from a distance or from fairly close? Notice the size of the columns. How do they compare with those next to Heston during the funeral scene? What is the effect of having these great columns next to a character delivering a powerful oration to the citizens of Rome?

Comment on the authenticity of the battle scenes in each film translation of *Julius Caesar*. How do they compare with similar scenes from *Ben Hur* or *Cleopatra*?

Productions

In *Shakespeare on Screen,* Rothwell and Melzer list forty-two films made between 1907 and 1987 from the play-text of *Julius Caesar.* However, only one of these (Wise's 1978 BBC Television translation; 180 minutes) includes most of the Shakespearean script. The earliest film, a 1907 Italian production, depicts Shakespeare writing *Julius Caesar.* Eight of the films, mostly shot before 1912, were 10 minutes or less; the earliest feature-length sound film was shot in 1938 for BBC Television and seventeen of the other films were also television productions, either in the United Kingdom or in the United States. Ten of the films were produced specifically for schools, generally short features dealing with theme, atmosphere, and specific scenes. A range of alternative treatments is also available: a Black-Hispanic production shot at the New York Film Festival; a comparison of four profiles of Caesar (Caesar's view of himself, Plutarch's report, and plays by Shakespeare and Shaw); a dress rehearsal of the British National Youth Theatre Company; and a six-minute sketch on the Bill Cosby television show.

If Caesar is only "a Mussolini-styled windbag," then the fears of Republican Romans are undercut and the issues are diminished. It is worth applying the same lens to Brutus, Cassius, Marc Antony, or Octavius. Are these men powerful enough to argue the affairs of state in the Capitol and to command Roman legions? Are they charismatic? Do they have an aura of command? Do they have strong bodies and powerful voices? Do their eyes "flash like the glint of steel?" Of is each of these questions answered in the casting and camera angles used to present them on the screen?

If various translations of the play are available, it is worth comparing the directors' and actors' visions in several ways because, for some viewers, the actors chosen to play major roles, and the ways the actors play these roles, are revealing. For example, Knoll examines Caesar as played by Charles Gray in the Wise BBC Television production. Knoll argues that the "Caesar of Charles Gray is fully realized if less forceful, less dangerous, than some readers of the play find the character to be." (Rothwell and Melzer, 124)

Parody

Some years ago, the American situation comedy *Moonlighting* did an episode based on *The Taming of the Shrew*. Interestingly, there was strong audience reaction to the episode. In the 1950s, the Canadian comedy team, Wayne and Schuster, shot a parody of *Julius Caesar* for the Canadian Broadcasting Corporation. This parody was also aired on the popular Ed Sullivan show "Toast of the Town," nationally televised in the United States.

Further Questions For Discussion

1. Both Mankiewicz and Burge present the argument between Brutus and Cassius (Act IV, iii) largely uncut. Both, however, cut parts of Brutus's "You have done that which you should be sorry for" speech (lines 66-83), but there are differences. Burge cuts Brutus's line "For I can raise no money by vile means" (72), but Mankiewicz leaves it in. What is the effect of omitting this line? Decide whether you think that Jason Robards' Brutus (Burge) would have a less difficult time saying the line than James Mason's Brutus. In which ways would the line detract from the credibility of the Brutus that Mason portrays?

2. There is more movement by the camera in the Burge production than in the Mankiewicz production. What effect does this camera activity create? An interesting technique employed in this translation is to have the audience see Brutus through the dying eyes of Caesar and, therefore, shift the narrative point of view. Why do you think this was done and how effective is it?

3. The Mankiewicz production is in black and white. Does this create any problems for you as a film reader? How does the use of black and white affect the setting (light and shadow for instance)?

4. What is the central purpose of the costuming in each film. What problems in costuming are evident in the black and white film?

5. The recording of the Canadian comedy duo, Wayne and Schuster, *Rinse the Blood Off My Toga,* is probably the funniest parody on Julius Caesar. It tells the story of how a Roman private detective discovers who killed "Big Julie." How is the bloodstained toga used effectively in the Burge translation?

6. When you have completed your viewing of both the Mankiewicz and the Burge productions, rate the films on at least five of the points you believe movie critics might use to judge each film (such as acting, cinematography, costumes, sets, sound tracks, film editing, pace, interest). On the basis of your ratings, which film appears to be the better production? Do your ratings calculations match with your personal response to the film? Which of the critical qualities you have used do you believe the general public uses to judge a movie?

   Develop a list of film qualities that seem to be very important for establishing public reaction to a film and rate the films on these qualities.

   Use your judgments to predict how well the films did at the box office and then compare your predictions with film awards (Academy Awards, Genie Awards, Cannes Film Festival Awards), with critical reviews, and with box office film earnings (all of this information is available on the internet).

CHAPTER SIX

Twelfth Night

Establishing Shot 1

No director wants to be associated with a production that is simply a carbon copy of previous productions. This is particularly so in the case of Shakespeare, where it is likely that a good proportion of the audience will have seen a particular play before. Hence there is often a striving for novelty, occasionally with incongruous results: a recent Australian production of *King Lear*, for example, introduced popular songs like "My Heart Belongs to Daddy" and had the Fool dressed as Shirley Temple.

Without going to such extremes, a feeling of freshness can be created simply by changing the period in which the play is set. Such a change also underlines Shakespeare's universality: relatively few, if any, of Shakespeare's plays do not permit the director such freedom.

Four film versions of *Twelfth Night* are readily available on video, two of them adapted from stage productions:

- 1980: Petruchio BBC/Time-Life Television version. Director: John Gorrie
- 1986: Director: Neil Armfield (Australian production in modern setting; distribution rights held by Australian Film Institute)
- 1988: Renaissance Theatre Company. Directors: Kenneth Branagh and Paul Kafno
- 1996: British production. Director: Trevor Nunn

The BBC *Twelfth Night* was one of the few in that project to win general praise. Neil Armfield transferred his highly successful stage production to film so successfully that it won the accolade of "notable production" in a British publication, *Shakespeare in Performance* (Parsons and Mason, 1995), as did Kenneth Branagh's and Paul Kafno's Renaissance Theatre Company production. On the other hand, the Trevor Nunn film, a big budget production, and the only substantial translation of the play-text into the film medium, received mixed reviews.

Director's Cut 1

Begin at the beginning? Shakespeare's play-text opens at Orsino's court, and we learn of his love for Olivia. The second scene shows Viola and the Sea Captain, who have struggled ashore from the wreck. Over the years, many stage directors have reversed these scenes, and in the film versions we are discussing in this chapter, two directors have taken the same path. What are the arguments for and against this change?

Setting

Each of the films/videos under discussion shifts the period of the play from Elizabethan times: the BBC version adopts Stuart dress, and much of the action takes place in two Jacobean mansions; the Neil Armfield version has a modern setting (a Sydney seaside suburb or a Great Barrier Reef island); and both Kenneth Branagh/Paul Kafno and Trevor Nunn have chosen the nineteenth century.

Time and Space

The action of the play covers a period of approximately a week. This raises the question, allied to that of setting, of whether a particular season of the year should be signalled. A production which gives weight to the play's title, for example, might well choose a winter setting (Twelfth Night was the twelfth day after Christmas and the final night for festivities). On the other hand, a director wishing to create a "sunny" comedy might choose spring or summer. Which season do you think best fits the mood of the play?

Both the Armfield and Branagh/Kafno versions, presumably because of financial considerations, have what are basically stage sets; in the BBC version, the camera moves more freely, and in Trevor Nunn's version for theatrical release, we are presented with a wide variety of indoor and outdoor settings.

Cutaway 6 Take 1

In a small group, view at least two of the four versions. Then consider whether anything is lost by moving the setting forward from Elizabethan times? Would it be credible to develop a translation set in a futuristic setting?

Dress often signals social status. In the versions you have read, what is signalled about Maria's status in Olivia's household?

In reading the Branagh/Kafno and Nunn versions, what differences to you notice in the costuming? Do these differences affect your response?

Cutaway 6 Take 2

Do you find the severely limited settings of the Armfield and Branagh/Kafno versions constricting to you as a reader? Does it worry you that, in the words of one reviewer, in the Branagh/Kafno translation Olivia and Orsino appear to live on opposite sides of a cemetery? (Note the surrealistic touch in this set.) Are there any advantages springing from such restricted settings?

Of the four versions under consideration, only the Trevor Nunn production was specifically designed with the large screen in mind; all the others were prepared for television or video player. In your group, discuss the different demands and possibilities of each medium.

One obvious difference, of course, is the greater use of close-ups in television. Compare the Trevor Nunn version with one of the others in this regard.

Establishing Shot 2

Illyria is the setting of the play, but one may safely assume that, to the Elizabethans, the name "Illyria" had much the same connotation as "Ruritania" has to us—a mythical territory. Hence it does not matter greatly whether the setting suggests England or Australia or, in the case of Trevor Nunn's version, an outpost of the Austro-Hungarian Empire.

The original Illyricum was the name given by the Romans to the territory on the eastern coast of the Adriatic Sea, in other words, modern Bosnia and Albania. In the late nineteenth century, most of this territory was indeed part of the Austro-Hungarian Empire.

Willing Suspension of Disbelief

Viola and Sebastian are twins. On stage, the two actors are dressed similarly, and that is generally considered sufficient for the audience to suspend disbelief. Film audiences, however, have long been accustomed to a greater "realism." Neil Armfield's solution (Gillian Jones plays both roles) contrasts, in this respect, with the decisions of the other directors to cast actors with some facial similarity and similar hair styles. In the Branagh/Kafno version, Frances Barber's Viola and Christopher Hollis's Sebastian resemble each other in looks, but it seems reasonable to suggest that Olivia "might" notice the way "Cesario" has grown in the space of a few hours. The technical flexibility of film suggests Armfield's solution so it is difficult to understand why the other directors do not adopt the same approach. On the other hand, some directors appear to be torn between their desire to hold on to the conventions of the stage at the cost of losing the opportunities offered by film. Sometimes these decisions interfere in establishing a credible translation of the play-text from Elizabethan stage to modern television or theatre screen. If this happens, it seems reasonable to argue that the director is providing a poor translation of Shakespeare's motivating need—to provide substantial entertainment for a discerning, and paying, audience.

Cutaway 6 Take 3

In what ways are the audiences of stage plays educated to suspend belief and not demand absolute realism? Alternatively, in which ways are film audiences "educated" in the opposite direction? Is the average film truly realistic?

Sexuality in Illyricum

Inevitably, in a play where there is a boy playing a girl playing a boy (remember that in Shakespeare's time female roles were taken by boys) notions of gender—homosexuality, androgyny—lurk not too far below the surface. Further, there is the fondness of Orsino for "Cesario" and the attachment of Antonio to Sebastian, a feeling so great that he ventures into the count's territory at great risk to himself. This potential for confusion has recently been illustrated again in the film *Shakespeare in Love*.

These apparently dramatic devices involving twins and females in male roles to complicate the plot also offer considerable scope for comedy and the case of mistaken identity is used in several of Shakespeare's comedy play-texts. It is used equally effectively to promote the view that an intelligent woman is quite capable of outwitting men—even in such a difficult setting as the courthouse (as Portia does in *Merchant of Venice* when she fools the judges and outwits Shylock).

Director's Cut 2

One of the decisions a director must make is whether to ignore or play down suggestions of homosexual feelings or to emphasize them. Neil Armfield took the latter course: Orsino and Cesario are shown sharing a large swinging hammock, to the surprise of the courtiers. Consider one of the other film versions. Are questions of gender given any prominence beyond the basic notion of disguise?

Stage productions in the twentieth century have increasingly made Antonio's attachment to Sebastian explicitly homosexual; in the 1930s Denise Coffey went a stage further by drawing attention to the fact that there are no lines in the play ordering his release. At the end of her production the lovers are so wrapped up in themselves that they forget about him, and he is led off by guards, presumably to execution.

Clowns, Fools, Fun, and Melancholy

The grim note struck at the end of Coffey's production reminds us that perhaps the biggest decision confronting the director is making up his/her mind about the tone to be established in any translation of a play-text to performance. The key characters in the establishment of that tone in *Twelfth Night* are Feste and Malvolio.

Feste, in these four versions, is played by Trevor Peacock (BBC), Ben Kingsley (Nunn), Anton Lesser (Branagh/Kafno), and Kerry Walker (Armfield). None of the actors plays the role for laughs. The nearest to a comic figure is Trevor Peacock who conveys the sense that as a clown he is long past his prime. The others are all of a melancholic temperament, an interpretation supported by the gloomy songs that Feste sings.

Cutaway 6 Take 4

One of the criticisms of Trevor Nunn's *Twelfth Night* is that Sir Toby Belch (Mel Smith) and Sir Andrew Aguecheek (Richard E. Grant) fail to raise a laugh. Is this criticism fair? In contrast, John Woods as Sir Toby and Geoffrey Rush as Sir Andrew are certainly comic in the Armfield version. Can you pinpoint the differences in their performances? In a comedy as problematic as *Twelfth Night* can be, is it essential that we laugh at Sir Toby and Sir Andrew?

It can be argued that a Feste who is genuinely funny would do violence to the play. Given the songs Feste sings and the lines he delivers, and from your reading of the films and televised play-texts available, is this a reasonable argument?

All four Festes are at various points of middle age. Is a young Feste a possibility?

Some productions have suggested that Feste harbours a passion either for Maria or for Olivia. Do you find such a suggestion in any of the film versions? Would you, as director, see any point in conveying such an impression?

Music

One of the differences between a stage play and a film is that background music generally plays a greater part in the latter. In *Twelfth Night* music plays a major part as one of the three dominant patterns of imagery: images of music alternate with images of the sea and images of love.

Director's Cut 3

Why do film directors require more background music than is generally used in stage plays? How important is background music in creating mood or tone?

In your group, analyze the use of background music, and the prominence and treatment given to Shakespeare's songs, in one of the four film versions. If you were directing a modern dress film version, what kind of music would you choose?

Malvolio

Some directors have conceived Malvolio as a comic character from the beginning; others see him as a character containing elements of the tragic. If the latter view is emphasized, *Twelfth Night* can become a very dark comedy indeed.

Donald Sinden, a highly praised Malvolio (John Barton's Royal Shakespeare Company production, 1969), sees Malvolio as essentially a tragic figure. His imprisonment almost sends him mad, and at the end his degradation is so great that "I believe there is but one thing for Malvolio—suicide" (in Brockbank, 1988, 066).

Director's Cut 4

Charles Lamb, discussing the role in one of his essays ("On Some of the Old Actors"), proposed that:

Malvolio is not essentially ludicrous. He becomes ludicrous but by accident. His is cold, austere, repelling: but dignified, consistent, and, for what appears, rather of an over-stretched morality. Maria describes him as a sort of Puritan; and he might have worn his gold chain with honour in one of the old round-head families, in the service of a Lambert, or a Lady Fairfax. But his morality and his manners are misplaced in Illyria. He is opposed to the proper levities of the piece, and falls in the unequal contest. Still his pride, or his gravity . . . is inherent, and native to the man, not mock or affected, which latter only are the fit objects to excite laughter. His quality is at best unlovely, but neither buffoon nor contemptible. His bearing is lofty, a little above his station, but probably not much above his deserts.

Do any comments about him by other characters in the play support this interpretation? Which of our four Malvolios comes closest to Lamb's conception of the role? Does any suggest to you that Malvolio's sufferings have made him suicidal?

Cutaway 6 Take 5

No two actors ever give identical performances of the same part, and, as Donald Sinden has pointed out, no performance of a Shakespeare role can ever be considered the definitive one. What differences do you find between the Malvolios of Peter Cummins (Armfield version) and Alec McCowen (BCC), or between Richard Briers (Branagh/Kafno version) and Nigel Hawthorne (Nunn version)? It is worth studying closely the various versions of the letter scene and its follow-up, the scene where Malvolio appears cross-gartered.

Director's Cut 5

You are directing a film of *Twelfth Night*. You are anxious that the bitterness of Malvolio's departure is lightened in some way. Invent some stage business (no additional dialogue!) that will soften this section so that the audience is left feeling that some reconciliation is possible.

Nunn's Film Translation

As the only version conceived solely in terms of the large screen, the Trevor Nunn version differs markedly from the other three. Note, for example, the way in which the character of Malvolio is filled out by having us see him first in his role of supervising Olivia's servants in their various tasks.

Trevor Nunn's use of cutaways, often less prominent in film than television because of the need for multiple filming rather than multiple use of cameras, becomes a feature of his translation. As a result, while the other three versions present the first interview between Olivia and Viola without interruption, Nunn cuts away from the main action to reveal a startled Malvolio and servants as the voice of "Cesario" is heard shouting ". . . cry out 'Olivia'!" in the garden. Later, we see a close-up of his reading matter, a magazine called *Amour*! Nunn also makes effective use of flashbacks, as when Viola ponders the meaning of the ring.

The greater freedom of the large-scale production has allowed Trevor Nunn to intercut many visual images of the sea. In doing so, he is able to create a translation in which the sea becomes a character in its own right, vindictive, romantic, and jealously separating the characters from a future they can only imagine.

The critical practice known as new historicism has focussed attention on the cultural context which helped shape Shakespeare's plays in the first place. For example, *The Tempest* was written at a time of great overseas discoveries and hence of experiments in colonization. A modern production of the play is likely to highlight those elements that reflect issues relating to European colonization and its effects, issues which still have relevance today.

Director's Cut 6

Trevor Nunn has not only reversed the scenes, he has also fleshed out the shipwreck scene by having Viola and Sebastian perform a musical "drag act" for the benefit of the passengers. How do you believe this affects the credibility of his translation of the play-text?

From a technical viewpoint, the interpretations of the four Violas, the quite different Olivias, and the use of black and white film (more or less) for the Orsino sections in the Branagh/Kafno version, all present challenges for the serious film reader. Suggest which solutions are most effective. Discuss the effect of using all of your solutions in a single film translation.

Further Opportunities for Discussion

1. Anton Lesser "gives the jester/musician Feste a mysterious rendition. Student audiences label him a 'burnout,' and he seems a man with a past" (McMurtry, 1994, 229). How do you see Feste?

2. "Kerry Walker's Feste was ambiguously androgynous, sang beautiful calypso songs in a very sexy voice, and spoke mockingly in a dry or ironic tone. Real menace was projected through the sexual indeterminacy which [she] brought to the role."—Elizabeth Schafer (in Parsons and Mason, 1995, 227). Is this an appropriate interpretation of Feste?

3. "Ben Kingsley's anti-social clown, Feste, is close to being the star of the show."—Sandra Hall, *Sydney Morning Herald* 23/1/97. Suggest some of the reasons Hall might have had for making this statement. Do you agree with her observation? Is it acceptable that a minor character should be seen as the star of the show?

Spatial Relationships

CHAPTER SEVEN

Where and When?

Establishing Shot 1

The second element of narrative film-making is called spatial relationship. Storytelling only makes sense if we know when and where things are happening and how they relate to each other.

In film, we can tell where things are because we can see the scenery and dress of the characters. If a person carries a sword and rides a horse then we will believe that the action is set in the past. If the same person looks and dresses like us then we believe we are in the present.

Sequentiality, narration, and polarization are important for us to feel that we are following the story with all of its complications, resolutions, and confrontations. To understand the story completely, we must also know when events follow each other in real time, flash back to past times, or jump forward to future events.

A flashback takes us back in time but we need to be shown or told for how long we have travelled. Sometimes the use of costume helps us. Sometimes the pages of a desk calendar flick past. Sometimes the hands of a clock begin to spin backwards. One way of showing a flashback is to make the pictures move out of focus and then back into focus in another time while music helps us to understand that time was passing. This technique is also sometimes used to show dreams.

Key Shot

A flashback is a sequence from the past set into the narrative present.

The historical positioning of Shakespeare in Elizabethan times is only helpful in making a film of his play-texts if the play is set in that time. However, Shakespeare wrote some plays as histories. Film-makers, like the readers of a novel, must decide on the historical period before they can develop appropriate responses to their reading. In the same way, Shakespeare's fantasies are timeless and many of his comedies were written as present-time texts. Whatever decisions are made about time within a film, the spatial relationships must be made clear by the film-maker.

Establishing Shot 2

Time only has meaning in a film when the film-maker shows the intended relationship between one time and another.

The usual length of a film is about two hours but the time covered by the story in the film can be hours, days, or even hundreds of years. The time between one scene and the next varies considerably. If a person is about to fall off a cliff or crash a car into a tree in one scene, the next may show the fall or the crash. When this happens, we talk about a real-time sequence. More often, we do not know whether the next scene is the same day or even the same week, unless the film-maker tells us through narration using dialogue or by use of a clock or calendar.

Although we read film very quickly, we do not always read it accurately during our first viewing because we are trying to connect other information at the same time. For this reason we sometimes lose track of what is happen-

Establishing Shot 3

Repetition is the retelling or reviewing of parts of the story which have already been told.

ing or where we are in the film. Repeating single images, shots, or sequences helps us to keep up with the story.

Repetition also helps us read the film in the way the film-maker intends us to read. It is harder to read the film critically because we are given information which supports the intended reading constructed by the authors of the film.

Cutaway 7 Take 1

Working in small groups, list some different ways to show that the time period has changed in a film. How does each way of showing time change work for the film reader?

In the James Bond film, *Goldfinger,* an atomic bomb is set to explode in Fort Knox in America and make the American gold supply radioactive. While James Bond fights the "baddies," we are shown the clock timer on the bomb. Although the sequence lasts for several minutes, the timer counts down less than thirty seconds.

Discuss the ways a clock can be used to increase or amplify the feeling of danger in a film. Compare the use of the clock with the use of music to achieve the same effect. Suggest why a clock would be a difficult device to use in a Shakespearean film.

Editing with short cuts, close-ups, and rapid changes of camera angle make time seem to move quickly. Editing with longer shots and slower camera movements—like panning—make the time seem longer.

Suggest how the use of slow, peaceful music with long shots may make us feel that time is moving slowly while fast, high-pitched music and short cuts can make us feel that things are happening really fast.

Write a brief article for a media magazine explaining how music and editing are used differently to show the passage of time in different film versions of *Romeo and Juliet.*

Cutaway 7 Take 2

Sometimes the opening of a film shows us the main characters and their relation to each other. It may also show some of the events that will follow. Work as a media team to view the openings or title sequences of several Shakespearean films. List the character names and relationships between characters which are shown in the short sequences.

Note ways character relationships are developed as the stories are told.

List any examples of repetition of events in the stories. Discuss the way characters and events are repeated in different stories to give a single reading.

CHAPTER EIGHT

A Midsummer Night's Dream

Since the seventeenth century, productions of *A Midsummer Night's Dream* have been heavily influenced by a "conventional" idea of how the play should be staged. By the late nineteenth century, the Victorian stage was overrun with fairies played by children in gauzy dress and dancing to the strains of Mendelssohn's music. The Warner Brothers translation to film directed by Max Reinhardt and William Dieterle in 1936 borrows heavily from this tradition. Not only is Mendelssohn's music used throughout (arranged by Erich Wolfgang Korngold), but there is also a lengthy overture and a play-out or post-lude of the music. At least one critic has argued that it seems as though the producers believe that this music has a life of its own; that it can be trusted to put the audience into the right frame of mind before the action begins.

Cutaway 8 Take 1

Felix Mendelssohn's music, developed as a response to the play-text, was composed in the nineteenth century. It forms the basis for the score of the 1936 Reinhardt/Dieterle film.

Research Mendelssohn's intentions and feelings in composing the work. Discuss the interpretation of Shakespeare's work underlying the musical composition. Listen to a complete performance of the work. Suggest whether this music should continue to be used in future film translations of the play-text.

In the earlier tradition, Oberon was often played by a woman, the mortals wore stylized Athenian dress, and there was a generous supply of thickets and wildflowers decorating the sets.

This narrative tradition was significantly challenged by Harley Granville Barker at the Savoy Theatre in 1914 with a controversial production that departed radically from the established stereotypes. Barker's influence has continued to be felt throughout the twentieth century.

Peter Brook's famous and innovative 1970 production at the Royal Shakespeare Theatre stripped away scenic trappings to present the play against stark, plain sets that included trapezes where various actions were played.

Establishing Shot 1

The principal productions are:
- 1936 Warner Brothers Production. Dir. Max Reinhardt and William Dieterle.
- 1981 BBC Production. Dir. Elijah Moshinsky.
- 1996 Royal Shakespeare Company with Channel Four. Dir. Adrian Noble.
- 1999 Twentieth Century Fox production. Dir. Michael Hoffman.
- Lindsay Kemp Company production. Dir. Celestino Coronado. Date unknown.

Establishing Shot 2

As with many of Shakespeare's plays, the stories in *A Midsummer Night's Dream* are borrowed and developed from earlier sources—many well-known his audience. The original story of Theseus and the conquered Amazon queen, Hippolyta, appears in the Greek legends recorded by Plutarch. It is repeated in Chaucer's "Knight's Tale."

At another extreme, Adrian Noble's 1996 translation, with a cast from the Royal Shakespeare Company, drew attention to the potential for stage actors to appear as "in your face" caricatures within a stylized and incredible framework when the translation to film is performed by an inexperienced film-maker.

Film and television productions draw from traditional presentations while introducing more contemporary elements in an attempt to enliven the play for modern audiences. Some of the imaginative possibilities of the play are revealed by these innovations while others become obscured in the production values crowning the interpretation.

Oberon and the World of the Fairies

The director's sense of the fairies and how they should appear is one of the surest indicators of what he or she thinks the immortals mean in the wider framework of the play.

Scenes involving the fairies in the forest occupy the three central acts and the initiatives taken by Oberon (and to a lesser extent by Titania and Puck) have a decisive effect on the action. As a result, how they are conceived and played has a significant effect on the impact of the film.

In the 1936 film translation of the play-text, child star Mickey Rooney emerges from a pile of leaves to present a cheeky, urchin-like Puck and there are several views of woodland—mostly containing small girl fairies dancing in a misty haze. There are some gnome-like musicians who appear to be enacted by boys. Their business precedes a decidedly melodramatic Oberon who rides a horse to confront his wife, Titania. His need for this animal seems to conflict with the notion of an immortal in decisive control of his domain. A reflective observer might argue whether such an earthbound character could really move in and out of his kingdom at will, much less have a detailed knowledge of what is happening in it.

In Michael Hoffman's 1999 film translation of the play-text, matters are very different. The scene begins with a similar movement of the camera through the forest to witness the activities of the fairies, but while some of them are female and have wings, few of them are children. Hoffman consciously sets out a range of different kinds of fairies, many of whom are adult men. Some seem to be gnome-like, others satyrs. Puck (Stanley Tucci) is a middle-aged man whose opening meeting with a bedraggled fairy suggests an attempted sexual encounter. He is urinating when Oberon confronts Titania with a movement of the elements (air, fire, earth, and water). This king, underplayed by Rupert Everett, has no need of a vehicle to move. He

Key Shot The details of the action which are left to the discretion of the director and actors are called "business." Business can affect our sense of the character or situation quite substantially.

shows a latent power that unnerves even Puck. This Oberon is decidedly younger than Puck but he is very much in control.

Tucci is not a mischievous boy like Rooney but he can also play tricks, as he does on one of the fairies drinking from a goblet—and later will do with the mechanicals when he gives Bottom an ass's head. Tucci's Puck has potentialities of his own for small pranks and larger anarchy; that anarchic possibility is easily controlled by Oberon but it is always there. Puck does not wilfully cause the misunderstandings between the lovers but he does enjoy them. He displays the more ambiguous, even malevolent, characteristics of the fairy that Shakespeare would have been aware of from Warwickshire folklore. A later scene shows a woman and a boy distributing booty to the fairies which we saw them stealing from Theseus's palace during the opening credits. This further underlines the ambiguity of the relationship between mortals and immortals, whose benign character depends on the whim of Oberon. It further illustrates the fact that the fairies, as receivers of stolen goods who do not quite understand their uses, do not maintain a complete advantage over the mortals of the natural world. The two worlds that Hoffman creates have frictions that were smoothed over in the 1936 film translation.

Key Shot The mechanicals may be skilled workers. Their equivalents today are tradespeople: plumbers, carpenters, and electricians. For the Elizabethan audience, they were weavers, carpenters, tinkers, and tailors. But they could also be people with no originality who moved like machines. As such they could be simple or even comical figures.

playing of Puck affect your appreciation of the role of the other fairies in the play?

Use these discussions to establish how each director is creating our understanding of Puck's role in the fairy world. Consider interchanging the Puck from one film with another. Suggest how this would affect the overall interpretation of the fairy world in the play.

The Mechanicals

The play-within-a-play is a common device from Shakespeare's theatre. It is even more common in framing the plays for translation to film (for example, Olivier's *Henry V* and the more recent *Titus*).

Cinematically, the major film translations of *A Midsummer Night's Dream* offer some illuminating comparisons in the presentation of the players within this play, the mechanicals. Perhaps too often, they are presented as yokels; as overly simple folk who comprehend neither the aristocracy nor the nether world of the fairies. They can be burlesqued for laughs but dismissed as a group of fools. This is essentially the view of Philostrate rather than of Shakespeare as he tries to dissuade Theseus from viewing their play. In fact, both of the films tend to present the characters as unattractively self-important.

All the mechanicals have at least rudimentary distinctions of character, but the key to their presentation lies with the depiction of Bottom, the weaver. Since he is the dominant member of the cast of *Pyramis and Thisbe*, his conception is a major influence on how we can respond to his colleagues. Both films make the interesting choice of a popular film actor to play Bottom. The Reinhardt/Dieterle casting of James Cagney, however, appears to have been less inspired than Hoffman's Kevin Kline. Cagney was a good box office draw, having made his name in gangster roles, but his talent for comedy seems less assured. He is directed to a staccato delivery of lines, which does little for Shakespeare's poetry. Cagney's Bottom is likeable, if rather ebullient, but seems to lack the depth needed for an audience to feel they understand him. When Puck places the ass's head on his shoulders, Cagney becomes more and more amazed as he feels it. The camera directs us to his shaking legs and we see the full horror dawning on him as he gazes at his reflection in the water. It is difficult to be certain, however, whether the director's intention is to create mirth at Bottom's expense or a sense of pathos that he has suffered a metamorphosis he will never begin to comprehend.

Kline is directed to a more delicate performance. In the rehearsal scenes, when he wants to play all the parts and makes solicitous suggestions, such as the need for a Prologue so as not to "fright the ladies," he represents both the eagerness and the literal-minded inability of the mechanicals to perform a creditable play.

Cutaway 8 Take 4

View the filmed translations of I, ii or III, ii, 123 in the Reinhardt/Dieterle and Hoffman translations. Describe the business performed by Bottom and by Quince. How is this business supported by the others in the company? How does this business illuminate differences between the two productions?

Hoffman provides a range of "fun" scenes. The mud fight between Hermia and Helena is one of the more memorable. Consider the value of introducing unscripted "business" into the narrative. How else could we come to recognize Oberon's underworld? How does it affect your understanding of the relationships between characters? How does unscripted business provide the director with room to build an innovative interpretation from the original play-text?

Even being doused in red wine while in full flight does not dampen Bottom's enthusiasm nor compromise his personal dignity. His scenes with Titania maintain this sympathetic view. Cagney's Bottom is easily carried away with the attentions of the fairy queen and having four fairies to wait on him. Kline's Puck maintains a touching courtesy and an ability to enjoy the strange situation he finds himself in without having the mental equipment to really ponder what it all means. Nevertheless, that potentially sinister side of fairyland already noted in Hoffman's translation has been made apparent when he first meets Titania. A group of threatening fairies arrives on the scene; he tries to leave but is lassoed by the feet with vines and dropped headfirst into Titania's bed. In keeping with the tone of the earlier film, Cagney at the same point is merely captivated by the attention and her beauty.

Cutaway 8 Take 5

Reread each of the scenes in which the mechanicals appear. How are they distinct as individual characters? What are the dynamics and motivations underlying their decisions to act the play of *Pyramis and Thisbe*? Establish a personal view of how you would like to see the play performed. Re-view two of the filmed performances and consider which is closer to your ideal performance. Write a set of production notes for directing your own version of the performance with the actors from one of the filmed versions.

Pyramus and Thisbe is derived from a mythical story recorded by the Roman poet Ovid, in a collection titled *Metamorphoses*. The story has similarities to the forbidden romance and deaths through misunderstanding developed in *Romeo and Juliet*.

In both films, *Pyramis and Thisbe* is played for laughs. This seems inevitable though it may not be entirely appropriate. They even share some of the business, such as the amateur actors being overcome with stage fright so that they forget their lines, the increasing audibility of Peter Quince's promptings as they make ludicrous errors, and the grotesqueness of their acting in both rehearsed and unrehearsed ways. Bottom and Snug the lion at times emphasize the mechanicals' inability to trust their characterization, as they think their audience cannot. The pivotal point in each film is provided with the death of Thisbe, to markedly different effects. Joe E. Brown plays Flute with remarkable restraint throughout the 1936 film. He gets laughs without apparently working for them, his callowness capturing an essential quality in Flute. His Thisbe, therefore, has her impact by working too hard. He overdramatizes the death, doing all that Flute does not do in real life. His burlesque emphasizes the efforts of the group of men who, while well-intentioned, are completely out of their depth with the play. Sam Rockwell's Flute, on the other hand, does not stand out remarkably from the rest. He has the expected anxiety about playing a female role and the usual difficulty at getting the voice right. Through most of the play he is a bit like a falsetto pantomime dame. But when he finds the dead Pyramus, he suddenly shifts gear. He delivers Thisbe's final lines with a moving anguish. Ripping off his wig, he dies with dignity, much as we would expect of Flute the bellows-mender. The superior smiles die from the faces of the audience and there is a moment of silence. They are unexpectedly moved. Hoffman's interpretation encapsulates that hard-to-explain quality in the mechanicals. It is small wonder that Theseus does not want an Epilogue and tells them their play needs no defence or explanation.

Cutaway 8 Take 6

When Hamlet directs his plays (Hamlet, II, ii), he points out that over-acting detracts from the purpose of the play. Instead, he says, "the purpose of playing, . . . was and is, to hold, as 'twere, the mirror up to nature." Despite their apparently comic abilities, consider whether the mechanicals should be overplayed. What impact would result from playing them as genuinely and appropriately concerned for the quality of their performance?

Romeo and Juliet is usually considered a tragedy but *Pyramus and Thisbe* is performed for laughs. Read the story of *Romeo and Juliet* and then review the tale of *Pyramus and Thisbe*. Suggest how the same storyline can be used for opposite purposes. If *Romeo and Juliet* was performed about the same time as *A Midsummer Night's Dream* was written, consider why such a similar play would be included in a later play?

Discuss the meaning of the term "parody" and then consider the need for audience familiarity with the elements of the parody.

Use your understanding of parody to suggest why the treatment of the mechanicals is important to an understanding of how *A Midsummer Night's Dream* is balanced between being a useful commentary on love and marriage and being a slapstick comedy on the same topics.

Marriage and Love

Hoffman's unusual decision to provide Bottom with a wife remains a difficult feature of that film. She has no lines and Bottom is at pains to avoid her in the public square. The director has created a wife and then generated obvious unspoken tensions between them in later scenes. It seems that she sees him as shiftless and henpecks him. This is an apparently discordant note in the life of the otherwise self-assured and resourceful Bottom. It also provides a dubious contrast in a translation which seems to be exploring the features of *successful* marriage. All of the loves in *A Midsummer Night's Dream* have problems which are resolved by the end though each of the directors highlights different couples.

The inclusion of the fairy world provides a convenient device for exploring aspects of marriage that exist outside socially accepted values. To what extent would you agree that *A Midsummer Night's Dream* is a thesis on different aspects of an ideal marriage?

Placing *A Midsummer Night's Dream* into its social and historical context, consider why Shakespeare might have considered the play to be relevant for his audience. Can the same arguments be used over four hundred years later?

Hoffman has suggested that Titania has marital problems and these justify her passion for Bottom. What evidence is provided by the playtext for Hoffman's interpretation?

The forced marriage of Hippolyta to Theseus frames the action described from the original play and the films accept this framing from its announcement to the ultimate consummation. Appropriately, both Hippolytas are uneasy about their fate to begin with. It is clear that the Reinhardt/Dieterle Hippolyta is brooding over defeat in battle and the fact that her coming nuptials are forced. This is equally a factor in Hoffman's translation though she seems to be further concerned by the Duke's lack of opposition to Egeus's ultimatum about the dispostion of his daughter. It is only when Theseus overrides Egeus on the discovery of the naked lovers (after first conferring with Hippolyta) that full harmony is established between the two.

This scene in Hoffman's film establishes the basic difference between the two interpretations: there is a much greater sexual *frisson* in the later film. Victor Jory's Oberon seems to be peeved with his queen because he really wants the changeling boy and because he wants his own way. Aloof and autocratic, he fulminates against her until the device with Bottom makes her no longer interested in the boy. Oberon triumphantly takes charge of him; then he takes pity on her and restores her to normality, resuming marital relations with great pomp and pageantry. Rupert Everett's Oberon is offended in much more than his royal dignity. Portrayed as a figure whose power is within himself rather than in his sense of role, he is not markedly different in personal appearance or presentation from other members of his community. But he can literally shake the Earth when he is annoyed.

Hoffman makes little more of the Indian boy than to establish him as the source of the lovers' quarrel. It is not an arbitrary vengeance that leads Everett's Oberon to anoint his wife's eyes so that she will fall in love with the first person she sees. Nor does he take delight in that person being as repellent as poor, transmogrified Bottom. Instead, there is a smouldering sexuality in him that takes delight in punishing Titania in this way. There is also a wounded tenderness that does not want to sustain the punishment and he pities her when it has achieved its intention. It is no accident that sexual congress marks the reconciliation of the pair when Titania recognizes that she really has been "enamoured of an ass."

Director's Cut 3 A *Midsummer Night's Dream*, as a play, provides a study of love and marriage. Within the study, Theseus and Hippolyta provide an image of the forced marriage, Hermia and Demetrius provide an image of the arranged marriage, Oberon and Titania give an insight into jealousies and, from the play within the play, Pyramus and Thisbe illustrate the problems of loving blindly and thoughtlessly. Identify other aspects of love that are explored in the film translations you are investigating.

Sexual tension is a significant element in the confusions and reconciliations of the young lovers. In the Reinhardt/Dieterle film, however, it is notable for its absence. Dick Powell and Ross Alexander as Lysander and Demetrius respectively appear to have been awkwardly cast. A popular screen idol in the thirties, Powell appears to have little understanding of what his character is feeling at crucial moments and his reactions feel inappropriate to the modern viewer. It is difficult, for example, to see why he is amused when Egeus threatens Hermia with death or a cloister if she will not marry Demetrius. Similarly, much of Ross Alexander's performance involves rolling eyes and broad gesture. What either of them actually feels for the female characters at most points requires clearer direction.

Cutaway 8 Take 7

Marriage is a major theme in *A Midsummer Night's Dream*. From a reading of the script of the play, consider whether Shakespeare provides satisfying explorations of the characters of Helena, Hermia, Lysander, and Demetrius or are they left as stereotypes of "the young lover—male" and "the young lover—female"?

How important is the issue of sex for the narrative development of the play? What are the dynamics of the four relationships depicted in the script? Identify the problems you might have in translating these dynamics to the screen. How has each of the directors addressed the problems? Consider whether each of the directors has provided satisfying solutions to your problems.

In the light of your understanding of the play and the problems of film translation, how would you solve one of the problems you have identified?

Puck, on the other hand, has a wonderful time at the couples' expense, especially when he creates the fog and leads them a merry dance through it. Yet both seem to be more petulant than truly incensed about passions that are of real moment for them. In Hoffman's translation to screen, Hermia's insistence that Lysander sleep apart from her is shown as the result of more than maidenly propriety. Both have stripped to sleep for the night and Lysander is ardent for sexual intercourse which, though she clearly likes the idea, Hermia wants to postpone until they are married. When Puck's mistake with the love juice leads to both men pursuing Helena, the resulting free-for-all causes all of the lovers to be covered in mud. The scene is played both for slapstick and farce and well satisfies Puck's verdict, "Lord, what fools these mortals be."

Cutaway 8 Take 8

Several of Shakespeare's plays provide studies of marriage. Among the more significant are *The Taming of the Shrew, Romeo and Juliet, Othello,* and *A Midsummer Night's Dream.* Each considers the attitudes of male and female to forced or arranged marriage, first introduced for examination in *Titus Andronicus,* and each provides for debate on the role of love in marriage. Consider why Shakespeare might have kept returning to these debates. Discuss the extent to which arranged and forced marriages still occur in society across different cultures, religious groups, and class divisions. Are such marriages necessarily less satisfactory than marriages based on the personal preferences of the betrothed?

It is significant that Hoffman ascribes these knockabout comic features to the lovers rather than the mechanicals. The arbitrariness of love is shown as both ludicrous and unpredictable. It is only justified in the resolution and even that is not inevitable. Both Oberon and Puck have to work very hard to undo Puck's inadvertent mischief and the gratuitous transfer of Demetrius' affections from Helena to Hermia which has helped precipitate the opening action.

Director's Cut 4   The films create a range of different perspectives on courtship, friendship, love, and marriage. One is suggested by the lines:

"Love looks not with thine eyes, but with the mind,
And therefore is wing'd cupid painted blind."

Use the play-text to find other descriptions of love, what it is, and how it affects the lovers. Use these different examples to establish what you believe is Shakespeare's attitude towards love.

If Hoffman's film celebrates the joys of human passion (all of the human lovers, like the fairies before them, end up in bed on their wedding night at the end of the film), it is also frank about the inappropriateness of the behaviour that can follow. In contrast, the Reinhardt/Dieterle film ignores this aspect but does not succeed in elevating the action above the petty squabbling that affords Puck great childish delight.

Despite the evident differences between these two translations of *A Midsummer Night's Dream*, there are connections that are equally important in establishing a comprehensive interpretation of the play. Several points in the Hoffman film replicate or are influenced by the earlier translation. Thus, in both films, when Bottom receives his ass's head, Puck has blown fairy dust on him to make it happen. Both Cagney and Kline feel their heads and the place where their ass's ears were to acknowledge gratefully their return to normality. Both versions of *Pyramus and Thisbe* involve a real dog getting out of control and wreaking havoc with the mechanicals. These replications provide connection between the films but, more importantly, they acknowledge adherence to aspects of the predominant traditions for producing the play.

Though the Hoffman film appears more adventurous, it is not always so—and it is not always successful in its innovations (for example, Bottom's "wife" has already been mentioned).

Such Stuff as Dreams Are Made On

While every production builds on or consciously departs from its predecessors, the essential narrative remains constant. Within the framework of the Theseus/Hippolyta story are the stories of Hermia, Helena, Lysander, and Demetrius. Parallel with these stories is the story of Oberon and Titania. Puck's antics provide the narrative link between natural and supernatural worlds and the misuse of magic becomes a narrative device for stretching credibility to explore human emotions and everyday situations in exceptional ways. Changing times and technologies provide access to new interpretations and the sometimes uncomfortable amalgam of old and new, of traditional and innovative, can be seen in other filmed productions of the play.

Adrian Noble's Royal Shakespeare Company/Channel Four interpretation (1995) adopts the narrative device of making the action literally the dream of a small boy. The film opens with the boy in bed. A copy of the play he has been reading is nearby. In a dream, he finds himself passing through doors and into halls before arriving at the beginning of the action in I, i. Heavily evocative of Alice's arrival in Wonderland, he literally falls through a doorway into bottomless space before arriving in a cabin and then the enchanted forest. But this is not an enchanted forest to look at. Instead it is a vast open space where isolated doors, umbrellas, and stretches of water appear suddenly as they are required for the action. The film draws on the resourcefulness of the fully equipped stage with its ability to fly scenery in and out, to rotate and truck sets, and to light the stage in different sections. It evokes the experimental features of Shakespeare's stage and Peter Brook's, but it is also like a dream in which the landscape may have no definite shape. Like a Dali painting with its melting clocks and surreal plasticity, the dream structure gives the production a wonderful fluidity.

Cutaway 8 Take 11

Changing the setting of a production by changing the period it is set in or the location may have little effect on meaning for the audience if they are unfamiliar with traditional settings. Hoffman's shift from the traditional sixteenth-century Athens to nineteenth-century Tuscany allows him to introduce a bicycle and film the scenery of a currently popular tourist destination. Discuss the impact of changing country and time period for your personal understanding of the play. Consider whether your previous experience of Shakespearean plays has any impact on your response.

Suggest whether a shift to twentieth-century Vancouver or Toronto would reduce the effectiveness of the production for you.

If you were filming a new production of *A Midsummer Night's Dream*, where would you set it? Provide a justification for this selection based on the advantages your selection would have for achieving your ideal performance.

Through a Glass Darkly

A striking feature of Noble's (1995) production is that Theseus, Hippolyta, and Philostrate are played by the same actors as Oberon, Titania, and Puck. As well as contributing to the dream structure, this makes an unusual connection between mortals and fairies—who tend to be discrete in other versions. It also provokes a sense of parallel universes in which one action becomes a reflection of another. In this interpretation, Puck's role becomes ambiguous because he is now the point of reflection in the narrative rather than the agent for cross-over. His place in the affairs of both natural and supernatural worlds becomes more complex as the roles of the mortals and the fairies are clarified.

From Noble's production, the mortal reality reflects or is reflected in an immortality which is both accessible always and forever inaccessible. Like Plato's perfect forms or ideas, which we can all conceive but never actually see, Noble crystallizes the essence of the narrative lines while complicating them beyond comprehension. The characters become like those in a Pinter play—safe within their accepted universe but forever threatened by everything and everyone beyond it. The connection of this filmed production with Brook's famous 1970 production at Stratford-upon-Avon induces a genuine sense of innovation leading towards film rather than back to the stage.

If Noble's production suggests parallel universes inhabited by people leading parallel lives then the potential for future productions is extended infinitely. The shifts between real world and fantasy world that are touched on in earlier narratives like *Alice in Wonderland* and *The Wizard of Oz* can be developed towards a boundless future where we recognize our continuity with all people for all time. Our problems and their solutions become timeless in the manner suggested by the opening scene from Polanski's *Macbeth*. Evil, as easily as good, can lie in the sands of time until a tide ("in the affairs of men") reveals them to those who can see and covers them again.

Cutaway 8 Take 12

Some critics argue that Shakespeare's works are "classics" because they speak to every generation. What has Shakespeare got to tell the twenty-first century couple about marriage? To what extent do the different film interpretations of *A Midsummer Night's Dream* support this view?

Dream or Nightmare

A bizarre filming of a stage production has been produced by the Lindsay Kemp company. Deleting almost seventy-five per cent of the available play-text, the production translates words into action and dance. Changes are made to the story—Demetrius wakes to fall in love with Lysander rather than Helena; the mechanicals perform *Romeo and Juliet*; both Oberon and Titania look like drag queens and Titania actually is.

Cutaway 8 Take 13

Is it reasonable for a stage or film director to change the narrative storyline of a play?

Choreographers interpret all narratives in terms of dance. Do you consider it reasonable to attribute a ballet to Shakespeare?

Mendelssohn's music has frequently been used in film and stage productions of the play-text. To what extent does his interpretation support the Reinhardt/Dieterle translation?

The relation between *Pyramis and Thisbe* and *Romeo and Juliet* is quite apparent. Does changing the play-within-a-play violate the rules for interpretation of a play-text?

At what point should an interpretation lose its right to association with the original play-text?

Whether or not the Kemp Company production is a parody of the original or a determined effort to generate a new perspective on the interpretation of characters, the production has strong links with the Reinhardt/Dieterle translation of 1936. The forest settings are similar, the Mendelssohn music is used, and Puck emerges from a gauzy covering at the foot of a tree as Mickey Rooney did from a pile of leaves. Whether or not the director, Celestino Coronado was seeking to interrogate the earlier film interpretations, he acknowledges that it has some hold on the production, that it deserves attention if not reverence.

Cutaway 8 Take 14

In some interpretations of the play-text there is a marked contrast between the look and playing of the scenes at Athens and those in the enchanted forest (for example, in the BBC production, the Athenian scenes are more static and enclosed, stage-bound, in fact). In Hoffman's interpretation, there is a more fluid linkage. How do you believe the two worlds should be presented? How important would this connection be to your ideal film production?

Maintaining three distinct stories and including a play without disturbing the narrative lines is sometimes seen as the central challenge to directing *A Midsummer Night's Dream.* What are the most important challenges you can identify in attempting to produce a contemporary film translation of *A Midsummer Nights Dream*?

Prepare a set of producer's notes in which you record:
- the main effects you would aim for in your production;
- the effects or interpretation you wish to avoid.

Tradition and Interpretation

If the Coronado production is not an entirely original conception, then none of the productions is. The presence of a strong sense of tradition in all of these films is an indication that such things are not easily shaken off. In fact, our reading of Shakespeare can never be an entirely individual matter. In both subtle and more overt ways, every production must establish an indebtedness to the past through which the play is transmitted to us. It remains the role of the director and producer to bring that play to life for a contemporary audience. This may involve reinterpretation of traditional ways of presenting the play but it must also embody attempts to draw on the present experience of the audience to strike out in new directions.

Cutaway 8 Take 15

Working in groups, evaluate the acting performance of each of the following:
- Dick Powell as Lysander, Mickey Rooney as Puck, and James Cagney as Bottom in the 1936 production; and
- Michelle Pfeiffer as Titania and Kevin Kline as Bottom in the 1999 production.

Some directors (such as Kenneth Branagh) make a deliberate effort to mix stage and screen actors for films of Shakespeare play-texts. From your own observations and research, list the major differences in the requirements for acting on stage compared to acting on screen. Suggest the advantages and disadvantages of mixing film and stage actors in a single interpretation. Discuss your suggestions in terms of the impact on a particular scene from one of the films you have been viewing.

The 1936 production of *A Midsummer Night's Dream* was awarded Academy Awards for both photography and editing. Suggest how the camera supports the performance of Victor Jory as Oberon. Discuss the role of the camera in promoting Dick Powell as a favourite screen actor of the period. In what ways is the photography used to promote Michelle Pfeiffer in the 1999 production? Consider ways in which the photography provides us with a focussed view of the actor's performance.

The 1996 Royal Shakespeare Company/Channel Four production employed stage actors belonging to a professional Shakespearean stage production company. Consider ways in which this influences the acting in the film. Discuss the advantages and disadvantages gained from the selection of specialist stage actors.

As the agency employed to select a cast for a new production of *A Midsummer Night's Dream*, you have unlimited access to the world's best actors. List the actors you would hire for each of the major roles. Provide a brief outline of the particular qualities each actor will bring to the part you have cast them into and explain how these qualities complement your understanding of the character.

Director's Cut 5

Write a review of one film translation of the playtext aimed at a junior high group who has never seen or studied the play before. Provide the students with sufficient information in your review to follow the film as they watch it for the first time. Include what you recommend about the film and what you would ask them to watch for or follow to increase their understanding of the film.

"*A Midsummer Night's Dream* is a much more complex and challenging play than it can possibly appear after a single reading from the playtext." Write an essay in which you evaluate the truth of this statement with specific reference to your preferred film version.

CHAPTER NINE

The Taming of the Shrew

This chapter will focus on the Zeffirelli translation because the Sam Taylor translation is difficult to find. The musical screen translation, *Kiss Me, Kate*, (available on videotape) emphasizes the romance but loses the poignancy of the battle between the sexes. The BBC television production starring John Cleese as Petruchio probably provides the best translation of the verbal jousting with Katherine that has been recorded. In this case it is highly recommended as an access point to the play-text for comparative purposes.

The Opening Scenes

In Zeffirelli's first translation of a Shakespearean play-text (*Romeo and Juliet* followed two years later), Hortensio and Grumio ride downhill through the rain on broken down horses. In the distance lies Padua, unrealistically bathed in golden light with a rainbow arching above—a fairytale town. The music adds to the romantic theme as the pair stop to anticipate the wonderful adventure that is about to unfold for them.

The reality of the main street is crowded, noisy, and dirty. The music is drowned by harsh street sounds. Drunkards hang in cages above the street; a whore prepares for her customers. Standing on stilts to increase her height, she adds to the atmosphere. Nothing is as it seems: the romantic is faked, the joy is masking sorrow. The fun is hiding tensions.

Bianca (Natasha Pyne)—young, innocent, and beautiful—attracts the camera's attention. She does not fit into the surroundings and is quickly shown to be well protected from them.

The shorter 1929 translation, financed by and starring the famous Mary Pickford, omits the establishing sequences and begins with the domestic violence of the traditional puppet show, *Punch and Judy*. Adapted (substantially) and directed by Sam Taylor, the introduction of Pickford as the shrew follows a slow pan to reveal her as a vamp, dressed in a slinky costume.

The need to find Katherine a husband before her younger sister, Bianca, can be married is presented in a scene of pure slapstick—even the cat and dog hide from Katherine.

Zeffirelli's introduction of Katherine (Elizabeth Taylor) as an eye peering through a slit in the shutters suggests she is terrifying, malicious, and

Establishing Shot 1

Zeffirelli's film translation of *The Taming of the Shrew* with Elizabeth Taylor and Richard Burton is probably even funnier than Taylor's 1929 translation with Mary Pickford and Douglas Fairbanks. Both couples were famous in their times as film stars and for their turbulent romantic lives. Both translations take substantial liberties with the play-text and both result in great entertainment. Shakespeare, we suspect, would have been happy to see his work drawing so many laughs from the audience. Accepting the need to entertain, Zeffirelli acknowledges his screen writers and then adds that the dialogue is "by William Shakespeare, without whom they would have been lost for words."

 Key Shot In a pan, the camera swivels horizontally to establish relations between objects or actors—or to reveal elements which were previously unseen.

Establishing Shot 2

The comedy of the scene reminds us that Mary Pickford was a star of the silent movies—her rough, uncultivated voice could not match her appearance on screen so she had little success as an actor after sound films were introduced in 1927.

every part the shrew of the title. Taylor's eyes and her intelligence become the weapons of her dissatisfaction as Katherine—both within the household and during her courtship and marriage.

Culture and the Roles of Women

In the play-text, the arranged marriage of Katherine, the older of two sisters, is a necessary prelude to the marriage of the younger and apparently more desirable, Bianca; the older must marry first. This socially accepted rule of the Elizabethan period cannot be challenged by any translator of the play-text because it is essential to the ensuing comedy—and its resolution.

The rule, however, is quite common among a wide range of cultures, both historically and into the present day. It seldom leads to comedy, however, since it becomes the source of divisive argument about the succession of family leadership (for example, *Henry VIII*) and about inheritance (*King Lear*). *The House of Bernarda Alba* by Garcia Lorca (available on film) presents a modern Spanish tragedy arising from the need for marriage of the older daughter. Amy Tan and Denise Chong present similar tragedies arising within Chinese communities (in Tan's *The Kitchen God's Wife*, available on film, and Chong's *The Concubine's Daughter*).

Apart from the social problems generated by the need to marry the older daughter before the younger, substantial problems are created at personal levels. No sooner is he married than Petruchio takes Katherine from the traditional marriage celebration. He justifies his action with the words, "She is my goods. My chattels. . . ."

Cutaway 9 Take 1

Petruchio's bath suggests that he is completely careless about his own appearance and hygiene but he has spent considerable time and effort making certain that he looks ridiculous when he arrives at his wedding. Are these two sides of the same character or is one part of the Zeffirelli translation inconsistent with the other?

The concept of women being owned by men has led, and continues to lead, to some barbaric practices aimed at keeping women in "their places" in the name of family honour. Shakespeare considers the role of the woman in marriage in several plays, particularly *Romeo and Juliet*, *The Taming of the Shrew*, *Othello*, and *Much Ado About Nothing*. In each, he explores the plight of the intelligent woman in an uneven marital relationship.

Without access to divorce and without social support, the woman may be seen as a prisoner, and possibly even a slave, in her marriage. Neither film translation referred to in this chapter explores the issue in depth although Zeffirelli's selection of scenes in both *Romeo and Juliet* and in *The Taming of the Shrew* suggests that he is concerned that it should be discussed. His treatment of Queen Gertrude and Ophelia in *Hamlet* (his third Shakespearean translation to film) continues that discussion.

Cutaway 9 Take 2

Using your research into the Elizabethan period, suggest how widespread the practice of considering wives as goods and chattels may have been. What social and personal gains might be made by the application of such a practice?

Refer to the Ten Commandments in the biblical Book of Kings, and consider the strength of religious support for this practice.

How appropriate do you consider the practice of ownership of one person by another in modern society—as a child? as a partner? as an employee?

If you were asked to translate the play onto a modern western university campus, could it be staged credibly? What changes would you make to the play-script and how would you cast the characters?

The Taming of the Shrew presents a highly intelligent woman with an astute wit who is totally unwilling to marry merely for money or position—unlike a number of the wives in *The Merry Wives of Windsor*. Katherine is seeking an intellectual companion and her behaviour estranges her from all suitors until Petruchio. His willingness to marry her for the value of her (now substantial) dowry suggests that his manner may be as unacceptable as Katherine's. His wooing is certainly not elegant though it establishes that his wit is equal to Katherine's.

Although the wedding is a deliberately staged comedy, which Zeffirelli might have cut shorter, it signals the beginning of a "taming" which is generally unacceptable in modern western terms. Seen as a lighter comedy in which two strong minds attempt to gain ascendancy, it becomes a period of intense comedy. Sam Taylor's translation allows Pickford to overhear Petruchio's plans for her and to thwart them as she pleases. His Katherine has a tougher role to play.

In Zeffirelli's translation, the camera seldom comes close to the characters after they arrive at Petruchio's house. Often it looks down on them. Occasionally it looks up at one and down on the other. This helps to create distance between the characters but it also distances us as film readers. We are forced to stand back, watch, and listen to what is happening. Should Katherine be sharing some of the responsibility for the treatment she receives in Petruchio's house?

Further Possibilities for Discussion

Key Shot All texts may reflect or even assume knowledge of other texts. This feature is called intertextuality. Sometimes the reflection or reference is very obvious—we often recognize the impossible love match of *Romeo and Juliet* in modern television dramas—frequently based on mixed-race relationships. But such intertextuality is not only seen in the storylines: the opening scene from Branagh's translation of *Much Ado About Nothing* deliberately reminds film readers of the earlier film *The Magnificent Seven* which, in turn, refers to a Japanese film called *The Seven Samurai*.

1. The most famous speech in the play-text is Katherine's apparent submission to Petruchio in which she describes a wife's duty to her husband. Mary Pickford delivers this speech standing behind her husband and tips a big wink to her sister Bianca to show that she is not "tamed." Zeffirelli shows a much stronger speech in which Katherine explains to both men and women what the duties of a wife should be.

2. In *Othello*, Desdemona's speech to her father about the differences between duty to a father and duty to a husband expresses similar sentiments but they do not suggest that she is submissive. Consider the speeches from each play and decide whether Zeffirelli's presentation of Katherine shows that she has been "tamed."

3. *Ten Things I Hate About You* provides an apparently adolescent retelling of the story of *The Taming of the Shrew*. Unfortunately, twenty-first century urban American high schools provide little scope for the complexity of the relationship that evolves between Katerina and Petrucchio. As a result, the narrative line is distorted and the promised insights fail to develop. Those seeking a more successful translation of this type will recognize the earlier translation of Jane Austen's *Emma* to film as *Clueless*.

4. The Taylor/Pickford translation closes with a feast—really the original wedding feast postponed. The music used is the student drinking song from the musical *The Student Prince*. This intertextual reference reminds us that the original intention of the suitors (except Petruchio) was to study at the famous university in Padua. Suggest how this musical reminder of the opening of the play helps draw the storyline to an ending in which all the characters have played significant roles in achieving closure for the production.

CHAPTER TEN
Othello

Othello was, apart from Shylock, the last major Shakespearean role played by Lawrence Olivier and he was reluctant to do so when asked by the Old Vic Company in 1964. The resulting stage translation of the play-text, directed by Stuart Burge, was recorded on film in 1965. The film record of the stage play suggests that Olivier was correct in identifying the problems. Orson Welles' 1951 translation is highly variable in both production and acting. For many film readers, the more recent Parker *Othello* of 1995 is the most accessible translation. This chapter focusses on these three readily available translations, recognizing that Burge's stage translation suffers from being a play recorded on film rather than a film translation of the play.

Cutaway 10 Take 1

Burge's *Othello* is essentially a stage version filmed; Welles' and Parker's are conceived as cinematic versions. Would you expect this to make any difference to your response as you view them? How do plays and films generally differ from one another?

Othello or *Iago*? Translation Problems

Olivier's "actor's sense" of the play is supported by the responses of a range of traditional literary critics. Their accounts of *Othello* have varied widely from A. C. Bradley's "noble Moor undone" by Iago's fiendish plotting to F. R. Leavis's "fatally flawed individual" who merely needs someone like Iago to accelerate his road to ruin. Either of these extremes has consequences for both Othello and Iago and each oversimplifies the complexity of the characters.

In Bradley's reading, an essentially good and simple soul is destroyed by a cunning, plausible villain. In Leavis's view, Othello's personality becomes more complex. As the drama unfolds, he touches levels he has never previously recognized. Iago, on the other hand, is reduced to little more than a mechanism to bring about the unravelling. Thus, for Leavis, the dramatic challenges of the play-text become more apparent.

Though there is little critical agreement about the nature of either Othello

Establishing Shot 1

Resisting offers to play Othello in 1964, Laurence Olivier claimed that in this century there had not been a successful performance of *Othello*. He also proposed that the play really belonged to Iago and that is would be difficult to present the Moor as other than foolish and credulous in the face of Iago's machinations.

Othello remains a problematic play which apparently presents its translators with peculiar difficulties in mounting a satisfying production.

or Iago, their interaction is pivotal to any translation, stage or screen. Both the actors playing these parts must see each of them in the same way so that they can strive for the same goals in the production as a whole. They need to preserve a shifting and tenuous balance between the characters as the play progresses. If they fail, the production is likely to collapse into an emotionally overwrought outburst in which the audience is never sure about what it is appropriate for them to feel. The common view of Othello as too jealous to be credible remains unbalanced in the face of a parallel view that Iago is too evil to be credible.

Recognizing this uneasy balance, a great burden falls on the ability of the actor playing Othello to show the complexities of the Moor through the poetry he speaks. On the other hand, it seems, Iago the actor must work in an opposite fashion from the intent of Iago the character. He must always complement and highlight the performance of the Moor to produce a dramatic tension that will be coherent and intelligible to the audience if he is to avoid reducing Othello to an incredible and overly violent pawn. Reviewing the success of the director in maintaining this uneasy balance is one way of evaluating the success of the three films under discussion in this chapter

Cutting and Characterization

Commercial television stations are often criticized for cutting films to increase the advertising time. This cutting sometimes removes dialogue and even whole scenes that are needed for viewers to understand later scenes. Film-makers are forced to cut the text of Shakespeare's plays to reduce them to practical lengths for theatrical release. Because of this necessary loss of text, *Othello* appears to present even greater challenges for the film-maker than it does for the stage producer. While the full resources of film are available to structure the work and to make dramatic suggestions, these advantages are usually only available at the expense of greater cuts to the play-text than are necessary on stage.

Cutaway 10 Take 2

Choosing one translation you have seen, explore how the film-maker compensates for the need to cut the play-text to create the translation. How are the losses of verse accounted for or replaced in the film? If you were planning a film version of *Othello*, what lines or speeches would you feel it was essential to retain? Which scenes and speeches would you cut? How would you replace them?

A two-and-a-half hour film translation of *Othello* must consist of considerably fewer of Shakespeare's lines than a comparable stage production. It may also highlight Iago in a dangerous way because there are sequences involving him which must be presented in detail to clarify the plot and carry the action forward, for it is Iago who is responsible for initiating the action.

Each of the three filmed translations tackles the problem of *Othello* differently. Orson Welles' 1951 version tends to be the most cinematic of the three, the use of the camera to create atmosphere and reveal the story suggesting Welles' earlier success as the creator of *Citizen Kane*. Since the running time is only ninety minutes (the full play-text takes about three-and-a-half hours to perform on stage), it is clear that the script has had to be cut substantially. Whole speeches and scenes are conveyed in a few lines. Welles relies heavily on the art of film to convey and even substitute for the art of Shakespeare's play-text.

Visions of a Warrior

Welles' translation foregrounds the havoc wrought by Iago and the torture he has brought on himself, to be enforced by the newly elevated Cassio. In the opening scene, the camera is focussed on the face of the dead Othello. His body and that of Desdemona are shouldered by pall-bearers and carried solemnly through the crowds to the funereal cadence of a piano. At the same time Iago is dragged through the streets by a chain attached to a collar. He is thrown into an iron cage which is then winched high up against the castle walls while Governor Cassio, sighted among the populace, looks on.

Highlighting the dramatic situation at the end of the play has the effect of emphasizing Iago's activity in the play. Audience attention is focussed on him as the most prominent living character. The director invites us to ponder his fate. The opening image, however, introduces an enigmatic Othello—impressive and dignified, but about whom large questions remain throughout the film. It is unclear what this imposing man really feels at key moments in the film, such as the temptation scene (III, iii) or the murder scene (V, ii). This lack of clarity becomes a fundamental challenge for us as readers of the translation because we must guess at his motivation. Welles challenges us to judge Othello but establishes the difficulty, perhaps the impossibility, of judging because we do not know—and cannot know—enough about the man. We must consider the translation after we have read it if we are to gain the same sense of closure that we are usually given in the cinema.

It is dramatically and cinematically interesting to see Othello literally putting out the light of the candle when he is about to "put out the light" that is Desdemona. What this actually means to him, however, is never really clear. Perhaps, being a warrior, he sees the two actions as equally necessary. Welles may be suggesting that he is a remote figure, as bewildering for the audience as he is for Desdemona.

Scene-Stealing—The Iago Dilemma

Throughout the Welles translation, Othello remains regal, imposing, and difficult to understand. In contrast, Michael MacLiammoir's mean and skulking Iago is a transparent knave. The vast difference between the two men seems to suggest it should be easy to understand what motivates Othello.

Cutaway 10 Take 3

Working in small groups, identify the features of Othello which suggest that he is a great warrior-general, a romantic hero, and an innocent victim of Iago's plotting. Use these lists to discuss the kind of person you believe Othello must have been. Does the result of your discussion suggest that he is likely to have been so completely tricked by Iago?

An opposite difficulty arises with the Parker *Othello* of 1995. This, too, is beautifully cinematic in its conception, making good use of localities in Venice (the film opens on the canals) and Cyprus. At around two hours, there is significantly more scope to use more of the original text, but even so, it is heavily cut. Again, much of the cutting takes place at what can be seen as critical moments in Othello's speeches; the motivation for his later, apparently stubbornly self-destructive, actions is lost as the director allows key sections to fall to the cutting room floor. Similarly, it can be argued that the cutting of Desdemona's key speech about a daughter's duty and a wife's duty make it difficult for us to accept her apparent passivity at the climax.

Cutaway 10 Take 4

Use the play-script to discover exactly what has been cut from Othello's speeches in both the Welles and the Parker translations. Discuss the value of knowing the full text of Othello's speeches. How does a close knowledge of the original speeches assist in understanding Othello's actions?

Parker's Iago is more prominent than the Iago of either of the other two films. Perhaps because Branagh is the best known of the cast, he is shown as a character with great charisma, a star. The director's difficulty in balancing the production is highlighted in this casting decision. Iago is a highly intelligent, self-controlled, and resourceful plotter who thinks of everything. We can easily accept, as we learn from Emilia, that he has wanted the handkerchief for some time. On the other hand, his direct addresses to the audience seem to suggest that he is too brash by far to have been trusted so blindly by the great tactician and general, Othello.

From the early scenes of the film when Iago manipulates three chess pieces representing Othello, Desdemona, and Cassio, we are given a clear message that this man is in control of the on-screen action. His ability to be what is needed with Roderigo, Cassio, and Othello seems completely confident. At the same time, he frequently stares at the camera after an exchange with another character to deliver a soliloquy which knowingly takes the audience into his confidence and reveals the coldness of his heart and his smug satisfaction in his own cleverness. The selection of dialogue from the play-script makes it easy for us to accept that Iago would resent Othello's preferment of Michael Cassio over him as lieutenant. It is equally easy for us to accept this as a motive for revenge. The unlikely speeches to the audience confirm his egotism as he breaks out of the film to reach us in our twenty-first century theatre seats—hundreds of years beyond his time—but they should also cause us to ask if this is reasonable in the translation.

Branagh's Iago is reminiscent of Woody Allen's romantic film character in *The Purple Rose of Cairo*; he needs to be both within the context of the film as Iago and in the confidence of the audience as the cleverest character in the play—a spurned protagonist requiring audience sympathy. From this viewpoint, it becomes possible to critique both the director's selection of text and Branagh's freedom with the role. Derek Jacobi has a more credible role as the narrator, Chorus, in Branagh's *Henry V* but then, Branagh is the star, the chief protagonist in his own translation.

The direction of Branagh's performance highlights the difficulty that Olivier foresaw. The sense that this man is so much cleverer than anyone else in the play helps the viewer feel that Othello has little chance in dealing with him. The casting of the lesser known Laurence Fishburne in the title role extends that interpretation.

Director's Cut 1

"From his first words in the film, Fishburne gives the impression that he would be more at ease playing the romantic lead in a modern tear jerker than he could ever be representing the imposing bearing of the respected commander of the Venetian forces. He appears to be more at home on the public battlefield than in the minefield of more private emotions." Discuss this criticism. Is it necessary for Othello to be physically imposing?

Parker presents an Othello with a limited range of responses. Even during the temptation scene he takes rather a long time to become worked up. We might expect a successful general to be used to making decisions quickly. The fact that the scene is presented as a series of vignettes in different settings makes it difficult to follow Parker's intention. What is the film wanting us to feel about Othello?

Director's Cut 2

It is Othello's physical success that influences the Venetian Senate and underpins his success in wooing Desdemona. Using the play-script together with the Parker translation, consider Desdemona's speech to her father about her love for Othello. Are the qualities which attract the Venetian Senate the same as those which attract Desdemona?

It is difficult to discover Parker's intention from Fishburne's performance or his appearance. As we see him, he seems abruptly, rather than suddenly, jealous. He does not respond much to what Iago first tells him and then he is fully convinced. This throws him into a moping distress where he does not appear to know what to do. As readers, we can become confused by his indecision. As viewers, we can more reasonably accept Othello as a seasoned general, a man of action.

Cutaway 10 Take 5

"There is not enough range in the actor's performance and not enough of Othello's poetry remaining to help us understand why Othello would kill his new wife without giving her a chance to explain herself." Is this a fair criticism? What evidence do we have to suggest that Othello might act without apparent reason to kill Desdemona in a fit of jealousy?

Even when Othello finally decides to kill Desdemona, we do not know what he thinks is his reason for doing it.

Cutaway 10 Take 6

Iago, Desdemona, and Emilia are in turn allowed to dominate what should be Othello's great scene. At the end we are presented with the tableau of three bodies on the bed and, for some reason, Iago snuggles up to them. Even here, he takes over what is happening! As viewers, we must decide whether the director or the actor is in charge of the film.

Discuss possible reasons for the inclusion of Iago on the death bed and compare this scene with the Welles death bed sequence. What are the major differences? Which do you find more convincing?

Characterization may be influenced by casting and casting may not be in the hands of the director. Big name stars and overall budget costs sometimes lead to strange casting decisions. The film translation of *Othello* may be more heavily influenced by the casting than by the screenplay. More importantly, the screenplay may be changed to suit the casting.

Cutaway 10 Take 7

Observe the playing of Cassio, Emilia, and Desdemona in a film version of *Othello*. Write a character sketch of each, noting the idiosyncrasies (personal mannerisms) of the actor and how these are employed to create the character.

Does the playing of each character match up with or extend your own reading of these characters? In what ways does the performance illuminate your sense of the importance of these characters in the play? To what extent does the interpretation of each of these characters interfere with our attempts to understand Othello's character?

Play-text as Filmed Stage Translation

The longest of the three films is Burge's record of Laurence Olivier as Othello. At 166 minutes, it presents the National Theatre production with most of the original cast and little attempt is made to adapt it for the screen. In effect, it is a filmed stage play though use is made of cinematic techniques such as close-up (not always successfully as Olivier looks very artificially coloured) and camera movement. Interestingly, very little use is made of music. Although the result suffers somewhat as a film, it has advantages in its approach to the play. There is more scope for Othello because more of his lines have been preserved. A very conscious attempt is made to locate the emotional centre of the play within the sufferings of the Moor. At the same time, Frank Findlay's Iago is a substantial figure who seems credible as the cause of Othello's anguish.

Cutaway 10 Take 8

In many productions, Othello is played by an actor in black make-up; Laurence Fishburne in the 1995 *Othello* is a black man.

Does this traditional view have a great impact on the response of the audience to the Moor? Observe the playing of Othello in each of the translations and consider what effect Othello's racial characteristics have on the film's interpretation of the play. What difference would it make if Othello were only a little darker in colour than many Europeans (if he were played as an Arab, for example)?

The Voice of Authority

Besides appearing in coal black make-up, Olivier worked on his voice to make it appreciably deeper than normal—perhaps in recognition of the power of Paul Robeson's stage success in the role in the 1930s. Olivier's voice has the effect of increasing his air of authority, as does the fact that he portrays the oldest of the three Othellos under discussion in this chapter. Othello's age, of course, has implications for the casting of Desdemona.

Olivier's Othello is a man who has been a professional soldier all of his life, accustomed to command and to enjoying the loyalty, respect, and un-questioning obedience of his subordinates. In the early scenes in Venice, which are much fuller than in either of the other versions, Othello can subdue men with a word or a look. When Brabantio, with his retainers, tries to apprehend him and take him to prison to be later tried for abducting his daughter, Othello takes command of the situation with the famous line

Keep up your bright swords, for the dew will rust them. (I, ii, 58)

It is not simply that Othello is fearless nor that he has men with him as willing to do his bidding as Brabantio's, but that he has the habit of com-mand. Brabantio feels some importance as a senator and as one wronged, but Othello has a just sense of the strength of his adversary and his own power in the state. In these public scenes, and also when he acts through

Iago's scheming to deprive Cassio of his lieutenancy in Cyprus (II, iii), Othello behaves with the confidence of a man experienced in military and public life. He knows his own value and how it is appreciated. He has clear expectations and demands that they be met. In these scenes, Iago is necessarily the respectful retainer, maintaining a façade that meets Othello's requirements. He is scheming from the beginning but at this stage he can only attempt to undo Othello through others: Roderigo, Brabantio, the Duke. In these areas, however, Othello is impregnable and Iago does not seem able to touch him.

Cutaway 10 Take 9

Discuss the difference in age between Olivier and Fishburne. How does it affect your feelings about their authority as successful generals?

Consider whether the Desdemona from Burge's film could fall in love with Fishburne's Othello. Which of Fishburne's characteristics as Othello are most important in your decision?

The Turning Point

When Iago begins to plant his poisonous insinuations about Desdemona and Cassio, he scores an immediate victory in penetrating Othello's defences. Act III, iii can be seen as the turning point of the play because the relationship between Othello and Iago changes. Iago's shrewd eye has detected the point of greatest weakness in the general—his inability to understand the range of emotional responses he is feeling in his love for Desdemona. While Othello is a good judge of soldiers, politicians, and campaigns, he is basically inexperienced in the subtleties of emotional involvement with women. He has hardly been able to believe his good fortune in capturing the love of Desdemona and he is particularly vulnerable because of the age difference between them. It is not just that she may find Cassio attractive but that he suspects he is ugly and unworthy of her.

Cutaway 10 Take 10

How does the casting of Othello in each of the three films account for the age difference described in the play-script?

It is Othello's emotional uncertainty, his immaturity in serious relationships with women, that Iago is able to play on with such telling effect. Othello's reaction is excessive, almost from the very first of Iago's tentative suggestions. Iago is able to become bolder as Othello swallows the bait until he comes out with his masterstroke, "Oh, beware, my lord, of jealousy!" From this point he has planted all that he wishes into Othello's consciousness. What follows, with the handkerchief and all of the machinations that attend it, proceeds almost inevitably as Othello loses emotional control.

In the first two acts, Othello is the assured old campaigner. He is the macho man, comfortable in command with friends and formidable in command with enemies. In the last three acts, he is transformed—almost into a blithering idiot in some productions. He has uncontrollable emotional outbursts (for example, when he is reading the letter from Venice, and when he cannot stop calling out as Desdemona is discovered with Cassio and finally strikes her, to the horror of Lodovico who thinks he has gone mad). Olivier's Othello expresses his loss of emotional control as a loss of physical control—a warrior response: he raises his voice, rolls his eyes, rants, strides around the room, rolls around on the floor, has fits. He has become the very antithesis of the cool-headed leader we were introduced to at the opening of the play.

Significantly, Burge shows us that the relationship with Iago has also completely altered. From being the trusted ensign with particular functions to perform (but not so trusted as to have been made lieutenant), Iago has positioned himself at the centre of Othello's emotional life. Othello now relies on Iago for his view of the world, for information about the most important thing in his life, his relationship with his wife. He is shown as powerless to seek verification from the person most able to give it. Maggie Smith's Desdemona intensifies the poignancy of this situation. She is deeply in love with Othello, bound in duty to him but baffled as to why he tests her so relentlessly. Her reaction when he strikes her, "I have not deserved this" is telling. Her restraint makes all the more obvious her husband's lack of it.

Cutaway 10 Take 11

As a trained and successful warrior-general, Othello sees the world in simple terms. When things are right, he does not act; when they are wrong, he must act without reason or mercy. As a warrior, this is his greatest strength; as a lover, it is his greatest weakness. Is this a realistic assessment of Othello?

After the murder, when he realizes the monstrous enormity of Iago's plotting, Othello is on the brink of emotional collapse. The neatly polarized world of his military experience is quite inadequate to his needs. The inadequacy of his manhood has been revealed. In his limited vision of emotional response, there is nothing left for him but suicide—the course he takes.

Director's Cut 3 The turning point of *Othello* is usually accepted to be the temptation scene in Act III, iii. View the scene as it is presented by Orson Welles, Stuart Burge, and Oliver Parker. Note how the scene is produced, the setting, the differences in the script, and how the play-script has been amended. Which do you find the most satisfying presentation? What suggestions can you make to improve each of the three?

In each translation of the play-script to screenplay, the contrast between the early Othello and the later is quite marked. The result of his personal weaknesses and Iago's ability to perceive and work on them result in the original controlled Othello becoming substantially lost. The difficulty of maintaining a balance between Othello and Iago makes it difficult to avoid melodramatic moments. Othello has to be both the cool public man and the emotional child. The contrast is extreme and, for film, the time is limited.

Cutaway 10 Take 12

View the conclusion of the three films (Act V, ii). Which do you prefer as a conclusion to *Othello*? Which most satisfactorily rounds off the thematic preoccupations of the text?

Identifying Translation Problems

The three film translations under discussion help us to identify what might be required for an effective translation of Othello from play-text to film. To date, it appears to be one of the most difficult plays to translate—perhaps because it contains two of the most complex characters involved in a plot which seems better suited to the action-epic treatment.

Western film audiences familiar with the Hollywood approach to filmmaking tend to demand easily understood emotional events because these take least time to develop and resolve. More complex emotional relationships are more common in British and European film treatments. Othello seems to contain elements which demand a sophisticated blend of the familiar approaches to allow sufficient dialogue together with sufficient action to create a satisfying translation.

Plan a film version of *Othello*. What are the most important features of the play you need to take into account in order to make sure your film will be a success? What aspects of the relationship between Iago and Othello will you emphasize? How would you want your actor to interpret the character of Iago? How will your actor interpret Othello?

Any translation will probably begin with a clear recognition that this is Othello's film, not Iago's. A very daring production might be prepared to minimize Iago's role so as not to cut Othello's, though the result would undoubtedly be a different kind of imbalance. A successful translation will use all that the play-text provides, including Iago, as well as the resources of the film-maker, to probe the elusive complexity of *Othello*. As with Polanski's *Macbeth*, or the Rosetta stone, the translator's key may lie outside the play in the complexity of loves, hates, and jealousies which belong with every man rather than with those Rambo-like characters for whom emotional development is always a crisis of credibility.

Director's Cut 4

The Welles, Burge, and Parker films each present *Othello* in a setting which corresponds roughly to that envisaged by Shakespeare. Consider the potential for translating the play-text to a different time or setting.

What would be the effect if all the cast members were black and Othello white, with suitable adjustments to the text? Might such a change assist in overcoming technical problems with *Othello* or would it create new ones?

Further Opportunities for Discussion

1. Why has it been so difficult for producers on stage or screen to create a satisfactory version of *Othello*? What advantages might a film-maker have in setting out to do so?

2. One of the great advantages of a film translation is its ability to use real places and recreate events in full scale. Suggest why Parker may have avoided a recreation of the battle and the storm which take place immediately after Othello's arrival in Cyprus. Discuss the potential value of this sequence of events for showing Othello in his true glory as a worthy general of the state of Venice and a worthy husband for Desdemona.

3. Observe the delivery of Shakespeare's poetry by both Iago and Othello in sequences from the three film versions of *Othello*. Whose interpretations of the two characters do you prefer? What do the performances show about how Shakespeare's lines may be interpreted by an actor?

While Findlay's Iago does what he can to enable Olivier to express both sides of this complex personality, Branagh's Iago leaves little room for Fishburne's Othello to change convincingly. MacLiammoir's Iago presents the third "extreme" in being too apparently obvious. Leavis's "fatal weakness" in Othello seems to be an even more crucial weakness in translating the play-script to the screen.

Use your knowledge of the three filmed translations of *Othello* together with the play-script to discuss Leavis' concept of fatal weakness.

Despite the credibility problems created by the coal-black make-up, the excessive posturing and the stage-bound production, Burge's conception of the Othello/Iago interaction is the most interesting of the three translations. The way it changes and develops acknowledges the shifting emotional centre of the play. Its speedy transformation at III, iii is the key to its success. Nevertheless it is not as satisfying as one could have hoped.

Discuss the opinion of this critic. Do you agree? The critic identifies obvious weaknesses and complex strengths then shows dissatisfaction. Is this a fair form of criticism? Use your knowledge of film criticism and of the film to write a response to the critic.

4. Write a critical review of one film of *Othello*. In your review specify the strengths and weaknesses of the film as a film. In addition, point out what it has to offer as an interpretation of *Othello*.

Sequentiality

CHAPTER ELEVEN

. . . and Then, and Then, . . .

Key Shot A common element of narrative film-making is called sequentiality. Sequentiality means that things seem to happen in a logical sequence.

Key Shot The logical sequence of most events starts at a beginning which has a clear cause and then moves through a sequence towards a logical end, which we call closure.

When Mel Gibson, as Hamlet, looks across his father's coffin to see his mother with her new husband, we know that she has remarried very soon after the king's death. Two events which are separated in time are shown in the same sequence but the time interval is distorted. The play on the stage must show us the two events separately because, as an audience in a theatre, we cannot be seated on stage with Hamlet to see the happily married couple. We accept the sequence of events in the film as believable. Without the play-text in our hands, we remain unaware of the time shift the film-maker has made in joining the two scenes. In the hands of a skillful film-maker, this shift becomes invisible because few of us view the film with the text in our hands.

Films that are poorly edited tend to offer illogical jumps in the action. They may even cause us to lose that sense of continuity that good plots rely upon. At another extreme, editing can create interpretations that are unsustainable by reference to the text. Comparisons of Puck from one film translation to another demand substantially different interpretations of the relationship between the fantasy fairyland of Titania and the "reality" of Oberon. The recent film translation of *Titus Andronicus* suggests that there can be a resolution of the racial conflict set up and then amplified through casting within the film. In a similarly wordless scene, Polanski's *Macbeth* suggests, in the final scene, that Donalbain will repeat Macbeth's tragedy by overthrowing his brother, Malcolm. Closure for the film-maker has increasingly provided potential for a sequel and Shakespearean translators appear to be as open to this potential as the producers of *Terminator, Lethal Weapon,* and *Jurassic Park.*

In a similar demand for logical sequence and ultimate closure, Romeo and Juliet must always commit suicide for love of each other but the methods they use are governed by the times in which they die. Daggers are no longer credible, guns are unlikely, and even vials of poison now stretch our imagination. Future film translations may need to resort to high-tech final solutions at the expense, perhaps, of the role of the priest if our expectations of "logic" are to be satisfied.

Director's Cut 1

In the opening scene of *Othello*, Iago is bitter because he has been passed over for Michael Cassio as Othello's lieutenant. He persuades Roderigo to reveal to Desdemona's father that Othello is making love with her. Because Roderigo is also in love with Desdemona, he is easily led into mischief intended to shame her and embarrass Othello. As a play, this opening introduces the major characters and establishes their relationships. Discuss the impact of the scene as the opening for a film.

Othello is a strong general with a long battle record but he is black while Desdemona is white. Suggest possible openings for the play as film.

Discuss the changes you would make if you were producing the film to introduce elementary students to the excitement of Shakespeare; present a showcase of Canadian or Australian acting; take advantage of the multicultural nature of the audience; or focus on the changing role of women in society.

(Key Shot) A third element of narrative film-making is called polarization. When opinions or objects are polarized, they are at opposite extremes of a possible range. Polarization is the essential element for creating dramatic conflict in both literary and film narratives. Without conflict there is no need for resolution (solving the conflict or problem).

In most works of entertainment, reality is changed to create a narrative that fits within the time and budget available. By reducing subtle character differences and lengthy events, polarization is used to cut time and costs while increasing dramatic effect.

The reasons for wars are simplified so that peace is polarized with violence; the extent and effect of crime is exaggerated so that crime is polarized with a need for detection and one police character represents all police so that justice becomes the clear opposite of injustice. In the real world, we know that these polarizations are often over-simplified, even unrealistic. We are all sometimes good, sometimes clever, sometimes successful. At other times we have "a bad day." In film, polarization can be used to provide happy endings, justice, and peace.

Most of us enjoy stories where things turn out happily in the end but happy endings depend on sad possibilities. Peaceful endings need violent events to stop. Like the cartoon character that runs through the wall or flies into the air in the explosion, we know that it is not reality we are watching but we want it to be like that.

Shakespearean audiences had to stand in the open during daylight to watch a play performed by actors using no special costume. The audience had to watch and listen carefully and they needed time to relax from tension. Shakespeare deliberately polarized his plays by interpolating comic sections in tragedies and common people in plays about kings and nobles. Most importantly, however, he included clear explanatory speeches which simplified issues by showing them as choices between clearly opposing options. Hamlet's famous soliloquy begins "To be or not to be, that is the question." He then presents his thoughts about the meaning of life as a life or death choice— to suffer life or to die (and risk eternal damnation— "what dreams may come . . . ").

Polarization is so common that we often do not notice it. Most films are expected to be about two hours long and, on commercial television, they are interrupted with commercial breaks so that their length is probably about the same as in Elizabethan times. As a result, it can be argued, the development of plot and character we are familiar with has changed little, although both the technology and levels of audience comfort are very different.

In plays such as *Henry V* and *Richard III*, the central issues follow from a confrontation between individuals or groups who refuse to change what they believe to avoid or reduce conflict—the issue is polarized.

Key Shot The central motivation or reason for narrative in a melodrama is confrontation between people who refuse to change.

Key Shot A tragedy is an event or sequence of events created because a character cannot moderate the intensity of a feeling or personal characteristic which could be desirable if not taken to the extreme.

Key Shot A melodrama tells the story of a confrontation between individuals or groups who refuse to change what they believe to avoid or reduce conflict.

When the refusal to change leads to disastrous results, the play is identified as a tragedy. Macbeth's ambition leads him to be greedy and ruthless. As a result, he destroys the peace of the kingdom he wants to rule over and is killed. King Lear is obsessed with being loved. His desire for love leads to the destruction of his family's happiness and his own death. Shakespearean tragedies occur because the central character, the tragic hero, refuses to reduce the intensity of a usually worthy characteristic such as love or ambition.

When the characteristic is less worthy of our deep consideration—such as the need for enjoyment or the need for speed—events resulting from a refusal to moderate behaviour usually create a melodrama.

Melodrama can seem very simple and childish when it is viewed from outside the event and some of Shakespeare's characters behave quite melodramatically—usually to create comedy. More often, the emotions they experience and the unlimited pursuit of these emotions leads them to generate events which must be seen more seriously. However, serious issues can be melodramatic and melodrama can result in tragic consequences. The similarity between the two elements can even be confusing. Love can produce comedy or tragedy. In *All's Well that Ends Well*, the jealousies could lead to tragedy if they were treated differently. In the comedies, Shakespeare's characters tend to learn from their mistakes and reach happy endings—or die. In tragedies, the inability to change, the tragic flaws in the heroes, leads them to their own destruction.

Cutaway 11 Take 2

We read about tragic accidents and tragic events in the newspapers and watch them on television. They always involve strong emotions. Discuss the difference between Shakespearean tragedy and media definitions of tragedy.

Suggest how a car accident involving alcohol could be the basis of a Shakespearean tragedy. Who would become the tragic hero? Is this a useful way of exploring modern use of the term "tragedy"?

In *Romeo and Juliet*, gang members are killed in the fighting between families, but they are not tragic heroes. Discuss the difference between a tragic death and the death of a tragic hero.

Polarization is important if we are going to believe that confrontation between characters or groups is possible. In a family argument, we need to know that different family members have different needs or beliefs before we can believe the argument will happen. In a war film, we need to know who is on each side and why they are fighting. The confrontation can be created by placing opposing forces next to each other and then bringing their stories together.

When the confrontation occurs, we need to feel sorry or happy for one side and not the other. To create this polarized reading, film-makers may show us the relationship between characters or groups before and after the confrontation. The juxtaposition of people or events we like with people or events we do not like helps us to read the confrontation as the film-maker wants us to.

 Key Shot Juxtaposition is the process of placing unrelated shots or sequences next to each other. The effect can make us feel uncomfortable but it can also cause us to think about connecting information that we wouldn't have thought was connected.

Cutaway 11 Take 3

Work as a media watch team to follow the juxtaposition of events in the second scene of Kenneth Branagh's film of *Henry V*—from his entry through the doors until he is given the tennis balls. Make a running sheet of the shots used and identify the juxtaposed shots. Discuss the way the juxtaposition helps to identify the power relationships between characters to create a single reading of the events.

When Branagh's Henry V delivers his "Once more into the breach" speech, the fear of the soldiers is juxtaposed against the fury of the battle. Identify the juxtaposed shots and discuss the way they are used to create a feeling of action at the same time that they suggest Henry will be successful.

Films about war usually show pictures of the "goodies" doing pleasing or happy things. Against this they show the "baddies" looking unhappy and doing unpleasant things. How is juxtaposition used to create this feeling in the Agincourt battle scene from Branagh's *Henry V*? View the same scene from the Lawrence Olivier version of the film and discuss the differences. Make a running sheet of the shots used in the sequence from Olivier's film. Label the juxtaposed shots and write a short description of the way juxtaposition can be used to create excitement in a film.

Richard III

In the last half century, there have been four major attempts to transfer *Richard III* to the screen:

- 1955: London Film Productions. Director: Laurence Olivier.
- 1983: BBC/Time-Life Television. Director: Jane Howell.
- 1990: English Shakespeare Company's *The Wars of the Roses: Richard III*. Director: Michael Bogdanov.
- 1996: United Artists. Directors: Ian McKellen and John Loncraine.

In addition, there is Al Pacino's *Looking for Richard*, a semi-documentary act of homage to Shakespeare, in which he says "It has always been a dream of mine to communicate how I feel about Shakespeare to others." His film includes interviews with well known Shakespearean actors like Kenneth Branagh and Vanessa Redgrave, and looks at the casting for a production of *Richard III*. The film switches from actors discussing the text to early rehearsals and then to scenes from a final, costumed version of the play. Incidentally, the claim that *Richard III* is Shakespeare's most frequently performed play is repeated here.

Clearly, one of the main aims of Pacino's film is to make *Richard III* accessible to the average film-goer. The background of the Wars of the Roses is explained, and key scenes from the play are performed. Several of these scenes are worth comparing with the same scenes in the other films. One has to admit, however, that the degree of self-indulgence exhibited in the film works against Pacino's aim: much of what we see should have ended on the cutting room floor.

This chapter concentrates on the Olivier and McKellen/Loncraine versions, both designed for the large screen. Some aspects of *Looking for Richard* are also considered, and the chapter ends with a note on the English Shakespeare Company's version, which forms the final part of an ambitious adaptation of the plays dealing with the Wars of the Roses.

Historical Setting

More faithful to the historical period, Olivier chose to place his film in a late medieval setting. The costuming, however, is medieval fashion at its most "Hollywood" elaborate: the women wear high conical hats with silk floating from the tops; the men have elaborate headgear and long pointed shoes.

Pacino, too, in the costumed scenes that we see, has opted for a medieval setting: filming took place in The Cloisters, a medieval building transported stone by stone to New York and rebuilt as part of the Metropolitan Museum of Art's collection. Since Pacino is not trying to film the whole story, the scenes that he does include are uncut, and are thus often closer to the original play-text than the corresponding scenes in the other two films.

In contrast, the McKellen/Loncraine film is set in the 1930s. The film was based on a highly successful Royal National Theatre production of the play, which was directed by Richard Eyre in 1990. McKellen has written:

> *The crucial advantage of a modern setting is clarity of storytelling. It is impossibly confusing to try and distinguish between a multitude of characters who are all done up in floppy hats and wrinkled tights. (McKellen, 1996, 12)*

It is clear, however, from his later comments, that he and Eyre selected the 1930s because they were "a decade of tyranny" —a time when "a dictatorship like Richard III's might have overtaken the United Kingdom, as it had done Germany, Italy, Spain and the empire of the Soviet Union" (13). In other words, they were deliberately creating historical resonances.

Cutaway 12 Take 1

When reading the McKellen/Loncraine translation, watch for scenes which are structured to remind the audience of events from the 1930s.

After watching the Olivier film, consider McKellen's view that a medieval setting is "impossibly confusing" to a modern audience. Do you agree?

In small working groups, consider some other possible periods in which *Richard III* might be set. What difficulties can you see in trying to set the play in the future?

From History to Play-text; From Play-text to Film

As in his other history plays, Shakespeare compressed the action and made other alterations to the facts as he knew them. (It should be remembered that Shakespeare was drawing on Tudor sources, which had the essentially propagandist motive of justifying the Tudor Henry VII's seizure of the throne.)

He made the Lancastrian Prince Edward Anne's husband instead of simply her betrothed; he brought Queen Margaret to life (she had been

Establishing Shot 2

Any director of play or film wishing to present Shakespeare today must decide on the period in which the play will be set. In Shakespeare's day, the history plays were performed in Elizabethan dress, on a largely bare stage, with the words alone signalling a past time. (It was only in the nineteenth century that directors began to strive for historical accuracy in dress.)

These days, Shakespeare's plays are frequently presented in modern dress, but the motivation is very different—it is a deliberate shifting of the play to another time. Branagh's recent film of *Hamlet*, for example, has been given a mid-nineteenth century setting; a very successful Australian stage production of *As You Like It* was set in the Australian outback of the 1920s.

Another stratagem sometimes adopted in Shakespearean productions is to use an eclectic variety of costuming in order to prevent the audience from placing the production in a specific historical time frame.

Establishing Shot 3

Even though it is based on historical events, *Richard III* is not a documentary. Shakespeare felt free to alter the facts as he knew them to suit his dramatic purpose; the directors of both film versions have exercised a similar freedom with Shakespeare's play-text.

dead at least a year when the action of the play begins); he had Richard slain by Richmond personally, rather than simply killed in the heat of battle.

Olivier's film translation makes a further group of changes, including the following:

- it begins with the final scene from the previous play in the sequence;
- Richard woos Anne over the corpse of her husband (in the play it is the corpse of her father-in-law, Henry VI);
- the discussion between the murderers of Clarence is cut;
- the role of Queen Margaret is cut;
- King Edward's mistress, Jane Shore, who does not appear in the play-text, appears wordlessly in several scenes in the film;
- Richmond's dream is omitted;
- Richard is slain by a group of soldiers, not by Richmond.

The McKellen/Loncraine translation, as well as shifting the story to the 1930s, makes the following changes:

- it removes Queen Margaret, giving some of her lines to the Duchess of York (played by Maggie Smith);
- the explanation of how Richard has managed to get Clarence imprisoned is dropped;
- Princess Elizabeth is brought into the play;
- it introduces Richmond much earlier;
- Richard's dream is greatly shortened and Richmond's dream is omitted;
- it makes a large number of other changes, including some modernization of the language (such as removing the "thous" and "thees").

Director's Cut 1   Shakespeare's play-text opens with Richard alone on the stage. He reveals his plans—"I am determined to prove a villain"—and then sees the success of his first piece of plotting when Clarence enters under guard. Why might a film director feel that this is too stark an opening? What is a film audience likely to expect that the audience in Shakespeare's Globe Theatre would not? What is a modern audience likely to need that an Elizabethan audience would not?

Opening Scenes

After a foreword emphasizing that many legends have accrued around England's crown (and hence that not all that follows should be taken as fact)

Olivier's film begins with Act V, scene vii of *Henry VI, Part III*, which sees Edward IV crowned. As the courtiers shout "Long Live the King!," Gloucester exchanges a significant glance with Buckingham. We see the queen with her children, and catch sight of Jane Shore, Edward's mistress. Later there is a royal progress through London's streets, leaving Richard alone in the coronation hall. He delivers the play's opening soliloquy, with interpolated lines stressing the number of lives that lie between him and the throne. The British film critic, Roger Manvell, observed that:

> *The total speech, played in a single six-minute take in the large, empty L-shaped set of the coronation hall, is spoken direct to the camera, some parts of it intimately, ironically, in close-shot, other parts, especially those which are almost paranoically loud-mouthed, spoken from a distance, the camera following Gloucester into the other wing of the hall where the King's throne is set, surmounted by a vast, pendant crown. Gloucester asks for our appreciation with his slyly upturned eyes, his knowing nods and glances, and the humorous delight he takes in his own astute villainy. But behind these attractive touches lies the sinister obsession of his megalomania, and the devilish pacing of his crow-like feet, shod in black shoes with long, pointed toes. (Manvell, 1971, 49)*

McKellen's opening scenes step back even further into *Henry VI, Part III*. The Battle of Tewkesbury is in progress, with news coming in by tickertape to Lancastrian headquarters, a country house. Prince Edward of Lancaster, having said goodnight to his father, sits at his desk, on which is a photograph of his wife, Lady Anne. He is startled by a rumbling noise. Then a tank crashes through the wall and the prince and his guards are shot. One of the figures in a gas mask is revealed as Richard of Gloucester, who goes on to shoot King Henry VI. McKellen writes: "It is appropriate that Richard's face should at first sight be masked—as are his feelings from the world." (McKellen, 1996, 46)

Cutaway 12 Take 2

In Olivier's film translation of *Hamlet*, the soliloquies are delivered mainly by voice-over, as if they are unspoken thoughts. In the film translations of *Richard III*, we are considering scenes where the actors have made the decision to direct their soliloquies to the camera.

For each film, decide whether the actor is talking directly to the audience, or is he talking to himself? Which do you consider to be the better way of dealing with the problem of Shakespeare's soliloquies?

There is a swift transition to the palace, where King Edward IV, his queen, and their children are establishing themselves. We see King Edward getting ready for the Victory Ball, but his ill health is suggested by his having to take some medicine. The difference between the murderously active Richard and his brother Clarence is suggested by showing Clarence as an enthusiastic amateur photographer (a passive recorder of events rather than an active participant). Another scene change shows the queen's brother, Earl Rivers, arriving by plane from America. (In the play, Richard detests the Woodvilles—the queen and her brothers—as social upstarts who are making the most of their new-won power; a 1930s equivalent was to make them Americans, echoing the liaison between another Edward and Mrs. Simpson.)

The Victory Ball swings into action, with a singer, backed by a dance band, singing a catchy tune with words by Christopher Marlowe. (Note the initials on the band's music stands.) The scene will remind many viewers of Dennis Potter's TV series *The Singing Detective*. Richard's opening words in the play become a victory toast to the king, but the second part of the speech is delivered in the men's washroom, where Richard can look at himself in the mirror. Like Olivier, McKellen has chosen to direct his soliloquy to the camera. But note the contrast between Olivier's six-minute take and the swift juxtaposition of scenes in the McKellen film.

Cutaway 12 Take 3

In a small group, look carefully at McKellen/Loncraine's handling of the ballroom scene. A great deal of information is conveyed about the characters and their relationship to one another, information that it would be impossible for a stage audience to pick up, apart from those sitting in the front rows. The scene cleverly helps the audience to sort out all the characters, but in addition it conveys the tensions and anxieties of the court. What do we pick up about the relationship between Richard and Buckingham? What indications are given of the court's attitude to the queen and her brother? What is conveyed of Richard's relationship with his mother?

Director's Cut 2 In one of the most startling scenes in Shakespeare, and one of the most difficult to make at all credible, Shakespeare's Richard woos and wins Anne in the space of a single scene (I, ii, 33–225). How would you, as a director, make Anne's yielding to Richard convincing?

Olivier's solution is to split the wooing into two scenes, thus suggesting a time lapse. The corpse is not that of Henry VI but of Prince Edward of Lancaster, Anne's husband. Anne, played by Claire Bloom, seems to succumb to Richard's sexual magnetism. McKellen has the scene played in its original form, but, like Olivier, makes the corpse that of Anne's husband. A careful comparison of the two versions is worthwhile. Does the splitting of the scene into two aid credibility? Does the background of the mortuary in McKellen's version strengthen the impact of the scene?

The wooing scene is also included in *Looking for Richard*. Here the corpse is that of Henry VI, as in the original play, and here Anne capitulates completely. How do you think it compares with the same scene(s) in the two films of *Richard III*?

Director's Cut 3 It is argued that the film director can control the audience's point of view and limit the range of audience response more effectively than a stage director can with a play. In Olivier's film, watch for the number of times the camera focusses on the crown and the use of close-ups, particularly of Richard.

Carefully view the close-ups of Richard in the McKellen/Loncraine film, especially after one of his victims dies, and also after his encounters with his mother. McKellen (1996, 23) states that he is seeking to show Richard's "inner moral turmoil." Does he succeed?

In your group, discuss the view of Richard that each film seems to wish us to take. Which Richard seems the more evil? Does either Richard seem the embodiment of pure evil? If not, what redeeming qualities does either of them have?

McKellen's film gives much more space to the queen, her children, and her brother. How does this affect our view of Richard?

And what of Pacino's translation? What differences do you notice between his Richard and Olivier's?

Director's Cut 4

In planning their film of *Richard III*, McKellen and Loncraine clearly felt the need to create a stronger counterbalance to Richard than is provided in Shakespeare's play-text, hence the prominence they have provided for Queen Elizabeth, giving her scenes that are not in the original play and many lines that in Shakespeare's play-text belong to other characters. In your group, compare the roles given to Queen Elizabeth in the two films and analyze their effect. Does Olivier's film lose some of its impact by not having a strong counterbalance for Richard?

Visual Effects

Note, in Olivier's film:

- the repeated image of the crown;
- the constant use of Richard's shadow to sinister effect throughout (and contrasting with Richard's reactions to his dream—". . . shadows tonight/ Have struck more terror to the soul of Richard/Than can the substance of ten thousand soldiers. . . .")
- the effect of flaming torches coming in from all angles in the scene in the palace when Richard receives messengers who all bear bad news;
- at the Battle of Bosworth Field, the image of the crown rolling in the dust of the battlefield.

Cutaway 12 Take 4

What visual touches would you select as particularly effective in the McKellen/Loncraine film?

Director's Cut 5

All texts reflect back to other texts, a feature known as intertextuality. Sometimes this is very obvious, as in the large number of films that remind us of the story of Cinderella. But such intertextuality is not only to be found in the storyline. In Branagh's film of *Much Ado About Nothing*, for example, the opening scene is a deliberate reminder of an earlier film, *The Magnificent Seven*. Are there any other ways in which intertextuality, deliberate or otherwise, can occur in films? What examples of intertextuality can you find in either of the translations of *Richard III*?

Film Music

In both films, music plays an important part. Sir William Walton's music was, Olivier thought, "a lifesaver" in helping overcome the film's weakest part, the battle sequence (Olivier, 1982, 162–3), though some thought it too melodramatic at the point of Richard's death. Loncraine's choice of jazz and swing at significant points, such as the song at the Victory Ball, creates a totally different emotional response.

> ## Cutaway 12 Take 5
>
> Compare the musical choices made to support our viewing response to Richard's choice of record as he contemplates the photos of Hastings' execution. Discuss the effectiveness of each musical choice in terms of the way it supports the translation of the scene.

A Note on *The Wars of the Roses*

This is a film version, difficult to acquire, of Michael Bogdanov's epic condensation of the three parts of *Henry VI* and *Richard III*. (The English Shakespeare Company took the play on a tour of Australia and North America after its success in Britain.) The film is certainly worth seeing, but its particular significance from our point of view is that, like the later McKellen/Loncraine film, *The Wars of the Roses* has a setting that begins in the 1930s. It ends in the present day, with Richmond's victory speech a televised press conference, but at the Battle of Bosworth, the smoke clears and Richard and Richmond are seen fighting their final duel dressed in armour, one in gold, the other in black, and wielding broadswords.

Further Opportunities for Discussion

1. When Olivier's film was released, it was generally praised, though most critics have found it inferior to his *Henry V* and his later *Hamlet*. The McKellen/Loncraine film, on the other hand, has sharply divided the critics. Here are two contrasting views:

   McKellen's performance is far more successful on film than it was on stage, in part because the proximity of the camera breaks through the surface armour of his icy characterisation. As in the stage production, McKellen eschews the traditional majesty and charisma associated with

Olivier, who flaunted sexual magnetism and athletic vigour in spite of his limp and hump. Though McKellen gives asides and soliloquies directly to the camera, as Olivier did, he rarely ingratiates himself; he is no charming Vice-figure but a haggard, sleepless killer. . . . [I]n the film his work comes across as more nuanced and complex. The camera catches his relationships to the other characters in subtle details: the amused affection with which he offers chocolates to Tyrell, the glinting malice with which he flatters Hastings just before condemning him. . . . (Loehlin, 1997, 75)

and

. . . a parody of Hollywood films, at times mildly amusing, most of the time simply grotesque—a shallow, meretricious shadow of the stage production. . . . As with other anachronistic productions of a script . . . we have two plays competing against each other, with the Shakespeare script a distant runner-up. (Coursen, 1997, 141,143)

What do you think?

2. Both Olivier and McKellen deliver their soliloquies and asides directly to the camera, and thus to us, the viewers. Do you detect any differences in the way they do this, and in the effect it has on us?

3. A scene that is included in all three films is the council scene called to consider the young prince's coronation. (Pacino's film gives the scene without cuts.) A comparison of all three scenes will allow you not only to look at the different interpretations, but also at the directors' use of close-ups to convey the changing feelings of the participants more subtly than is possible on stage. Which of the three do you consider the most successful?

4. Do you think Pacino has succeeded in his attempt to make Shakespeare accessible to the average filmgoer?

5. For a parodied version of *Richard III*, see Neil Simon's film, *The Goodbye Girl*.

CHAPTER THIRTEEN

King Lear

Establishing Shot 1

Although scholars and critics view King Lear as a complex and rewarding play, many audiences have described the play as "dark, treacherous and painful." Directors, too, have different versions of the play, ranging from Peter Brook's 1969 "bleak and existential" television version, dubbed "the night of the living dead" by Pauline Kael, to Michael Elliott's 1984 version, described as a "symphonic poem, which focusses on Lear's suffering and the understandings and changes in attitude that Lear arrives at through this suffering" (Rothwell and Melzer, 135).

On a more positive note, O'Brien (1982) describes Lear as ". . . everyman with a common history."

The discussion in this chapter explores three film versions of *King Lear*: the Peter Brook and Michael Elliott versions noted in the Establishing Shot, and an earlier version, also by Brook (1953) that stars Orson Welles (who has also acted in film translations of *Macbeth* and *Othello*). As you view multiple versions of *King Lear*, judge which directors and leading actors have the best sense of the sympathy with human suffering which O'Brien sees as central to the play.

Sympathy with Lear is sympathy with the particularity of human suffering, human folly, human need, human bewilderment. Lear gains as much wisdom as a man can gain, without losing a jot of his individuality. . . . His simplest utterances open a shaft to the depths of experience (O'Brien, 1982, 76).

Directors

While films are frequently known by their stars—the "Lawrence Olivier *Hamlet*," the "Marlon Brando *Julius Caesar*," or the "Mel Gibson *Hamlet*,"—it is the director's vision that provides the foundation for the translation of the play-text to film.

Years may pass between the moment the director or producer has the initial idea for a film and its opening week in the theatre. Because of lengthy production schedules and because any individual movie provides a director with the opportunity to present only a part of his or her world vision (or *Weltanschauung*), directors seldom produce two different versions of the same play or film script.

King Lear, however, is an exception. Two of the three major film versions of this play were directed by Peter Brook. The 1953 version, co-directed with Andrew McCullough, was made for television viewing and starred Orson Welles (who shortly afterwards directed his own version of *Macbeth*). The 1969 film version starred Paul Schofield.

Brook's twin interpretations provide a rare opportunity to examine how a director's vision of the play has changed over the years, how the film techniques he uses have developed and grown and, incidentally, how television filming for a small screen is necessarily different from cinematic filming for a large screen.

In this chapter, we explore Peter Brook's changing conception of the overall effect of the play (if this were the same for both versions, there would be no need for the second version); his differing use of settings, costumes, sound, and music; the impact of casting on interpretation; and his use of techniques such as camera angles and close-ups.

At the same time, the third major film version—directed by Michael Elliott and starring Sir Lawrence Olivier—provides contrasts in both technique and vision.

Director's Cut 1 The social context of Britain changed substantially between the two Brook translations. Recovery from damage caused by extensive bombing during World War II and an even slower economic recovery left many feeling that their lives were irrevocably changed. By 1969, post-war recovery had taken place and a new generation was demanding an end to Britain's participation in the nuclear arms race, an improved distribution of wealth, and a new social order. In this context, consider the choices the director has made: black and white or colour? the use of horse-drawn carriages? *King Lear* set in mid-winter? In addition, it is worth looking at the various ways the director adapted Shakespeare's play-text. Are the directors' cuts similar in the two versions? Are scenes or parts of scenes presented in a different order?

The Divine Right of Kings

Before exploring the three film productions in detail, it is worth noting the exalted position of the king. In each of the three film versions, his absolute authority over all matters within the kingdom is evident. However, each of the three films uses a different way of demonstrating the power the king exerts over his subjects.

In modern democracies, when leaders retire, others rise immediately and apparently naturally to take their places. However, in Lear's time—and to a lesser extent in Shakespeare's time—the monarch held absolute power and the fortunes of the country depended almost entirely on the decisions made by him or her. The orderly succession of power from one ruler to the next, then, was of life-and-death concern to all of the rulers' subjects. The savage unrest and uncertainty caused by the replacement of the Catholic Queen Mary with the Protestant Queen Elizabeth is clearly portrayed in the recent film *Elizabeth* (1998) and the legalization of divorce by Henry VIII would have been very clear in the minds of the Shakespearean audience.

At a point in western history when the president of the United States can be impeached for lying about his personal behaviour at the same time as he is directing one of the most advanced armed forces in the world, it is important that, as modern audiences, we are reminded of the absolute authority of the monarch from whose edicts there is no appeal. We need to recall the Queen of Hearts in Lewis Carroll's *Alice in Wonderland* whose favourite line when anyone displeased her was "Off with his head." Two of Henry VIII's wives were beheaded for displeasing their husband.

Two obvious examples of the king's power found in the *Lear* script are the banishment of Kent and Lear's authority to divide up the kingdom without apparently consulting with anyone. Since he owns the country, he can divide it in any way he sees fit.

While each director works with the same basic facts, the visual medium of film affords many opportunities to either emphasize or minimize the absolute power of the ruler. We note below several ways that each director emphasizes the king's authority—for example, in the 1969 Brook/Schofield production, those who the king authorizes to speak are passed the orb—but you should be on the lookout for other subtle indicators as you view the various versions (for example, what is the effect of Kent being commanded to kneel in the Brook/Schofield version?).

Initial Impressions of a King

Most of the revealing comparisons and contrasts in the three film versions of *King Lear* can be gathered from a careful examination of the first act. Indeed, if you were preparing for a test and didn't have time to reread an entire play or novel, it could be useful to review the first act or chapter: what will happen in the remainder of the play or novel is almost always set up in the opening scenes and lines.

Initial impressions of characters in films and plays—much as initial impressions of people in life—come from their physical appearance, their attire, their speech (both what they say and how they say it), and other people's reactions to them.

In all three major film versions, when we first meet the king, he is bearded and speaks with authority. People listen carefully to him; all attention is on him. However, each film presents a somewhat different Lear, too.

Cutaway 13 Take 4

In the Brook/Schofield translation, what is the effect of the close-up of Lear's face, lighted from the front and top, surrounded by darkness? What is the effect of the mid-shot in the Brook/Welles translation?

Comment on the camera angles which precede the appearance of Lear in each translation: what is the effect of panning across the unemo-

In the Brook/Welles translation, the camera enters the throne room from behind, revealing a huge slab of rock which turns out to be the back of the throne; in the background, people are seated. What is the effect of this image? As is noted below, the Elliott/Olivier translation illustrates the respect commanded by Lear in a very striking image of nobility paying homage to Lear.

Reactions to Royalty

In the Elliott/Olivier translation, true to Shakespeare's play-text, we are introduced to the king by two nobles and the illegitimate son of one of them. They are making small talk while waiting for the king to arrive. It is clear from their conversation that, similarly to modern government press conferences, the king's impending announcement is an open secret.

As a result, we need to think carefully about how the film-maker expects us to feel about Lear in the following scene. Elliott shows us the nobles—and every noble in the room, including the king's daughters lie prostrate, flat on their stomachs, faces on the ground. Their arms are outstretched towards the king as he mounts the throne.

It is interesting to speculate on how Shakespeare's theatre company would have shown Lear's absolute power on the stage of the Globe Theatre (or maybe he would not need to do so, since all theatre-goers would be intimately acquainted with the absolute powers of the monarch and the need to show obedience in various ways).

Cutaway 13 Take 5

Research histories of England to explore whether prostration as a method of showing obeisance was used in England. It is useful to view the first entrance of Branagh's *Henry V* into his court for a comparison of ways in which the camera can be used as a character to create a sense of a king's power.

In other translations, the trappings of majesty are also evident. In the Brook/Welles version, it is assumed that the king has the right to speak. Before any other characters—including the king's daughters—can speak, however, they must be granted the authority to do so by being passed the orb, which they hold in front of them. Note Lear's response when Kent violates this rule of the speaker and blurts out his challenge to Lear's division of the kingdom.

Cutaway 13 Take 6

What other indicators of the power of the king do you find in the film translations that are not written in Shakespeare's script? Research the ongoing symbolism of maces, orbs, sceptres, and talking sticks. Present your research findings as a poster including pictorial and written findings.

The hall scene at Albany's palace (I, iv) provides insights into the directors' views of Lear's character. As we watch Welles (Brook's first Lear) interact with his men, we observe the relationship he has with them. This contrasts sharply with the character of the Lears in other film versions. It is useful to discuss the physical distance between Lear and his men, the differences in the way that the knights and squires speak to each Lear, Lear's warmth towards his knights and squires, and even the physical proximity of the Fool.

Cutaway 13 Take 7

Do the costumes worn by Lear in the different productions make a difference to the way we view his character?

Which Lear seems to have been most succesful at carrying out Lear's purpose "To shake all cares and business of our age/Conferring them on younger strengths while we/Unburthen'd crawl toward death?" (I, i, 40–43)

What is the effect of having Lear race his horse across the winter landscape in the Brook/Schofield version?

If you have access to other film versions of *King Lear*, use the criteria above to contrast the image of Lear in the initial throne room scene with Lear in the hall at Albany's palace.

Lear's Voice

In each of these three translations, Lear is played by a world-famous actor well advanced in his career. Therefore, we can assume that each actor (in consultation with his director) has given considerable thought to how he will use his voice to build an initial impression of Lear. Close your eyes and listen to the voice of King Lear at the opening of each version.

Notice how each actor strikes the tricky balance between the Lear who appears to have grown weary of managing the kingdom (the occasion in the first scene is, after all, the announcement of the absolute monarch's impending retirement to the good life of hunting and male bonding) and the Lear whose voice was the difference between life and death, between the security of belonging to the commonwealth and the perils of banishment?

Cutaway 13 Take 8

Develop a set of criteria on which to judge voice (for example, rate of delivery, volume of voice, strength of voice, use of pauses, deliberateness, timbre, and resonance) and apply these to as many film versions of *King Lear* as you can.

Supporting a Tragic Hero

To establish a credible translation of the Shakespearean play-text, the supporting actors need to be established economically and early, capturing the audience's attention, presenting their credentials, creating acting space for themselves, and providing a context within which Lear will be able to generate the seeds of his own destruction. In *King Lear*, four characters are usually singled out for attention—Regan, Goneril, Cordelia, and Albany.

In any complex translation of *King Lear*, the roles of apparently lesser characters such as the Fool, Edgar, Kent, Edmund, and Cornwall can be used to strengthen or weaken the effect of more substantial characters. The role of the fool in Elizabethan theatre is particularly critical (for further detail, see the discussion of the Fool in the chapter on *Twelfth Night*). Keep in mind, of course, that plays and films can be enhanced or marred by the performances of even relatively minor supporting characters (consider Jack Lemmon in Branagh's *Hamlet*).

Goneril is the first sister asked to profess her love for her father, but each of the three actresses playing Goneril (Beatrice Straight in Brook/Welles, Irene Worth in Brook/Schofield, and Dorothy Tutin in Elliott/Olivier) presents a somewhat different princess. All three have very similar lines to deliver, but their appearances (the way each wears her hair; their costumes and jewellery), demeanours (postures, movements, facial expressions), and voices (tone, pitch, rate of presentation) demonstrate different interpretations of the character.

Sexuality in Lear

Under Elliott's direction, Goneril and Regan each shows tendencies towards inappropriate sexual behaviour early in the film. Goneril, for example, at the beginning of the hall scene in Albany's palace, appears to be flirting with her servant Oswald. The inappropriate sexual behaviour of Goneril and Regan begins later in the play in both of Brook's translations.

Regan, as the middle child of three in her family, would probably have needed to work hard to set herself apart from her sisters. In all three translations of Lear, Regan is introduced as the middle child, the one who is left to repeat her older sister's praises, adding what she can, one not in line for the "more opulent third" to be given her younger sister. It is, however, worth contrasting Diana Rigg's Regan (Elliott/Olivier) with those of the two Brook translations (Margaret Phillips in Brook/Welles, Susan Engel in Brook/Schofield).

What words might be used to characterize the relationship between Lear and Regan in the Elliott/Olivier translation as Lear motions to her to demonstrate her subservience? What do you notice about Lear's and Regan's facial expressions? While Shakespeare's script does not suggest this, Elliott clearly felt that it contributed to the film. Is it an innocent, light-hearted game between father and daughter, or is there something more sinister being implied here?

Possibly the most rewarding contrasts between the translations are the initial images of Cordelia in the Brook/Schofield translation because her asides are omitted from the opening scene. As a result, we are deprived of her initial thoughts and forced to evaluate our reaction to her on the basis of her appearance and those cutaway shots which allow us to see how she sees others at court and how they see her.

Contrast the initial throne room scene in this translation with at least one other translation to examine the initial believability of Cordelia. Which Cordelia seems more genuine?

What is gained by omitting Cordelia's asides? Contrast the Brook/Schofield Cordelia (Anne-lise Gabold) with the Brook/Welles Cordelia (Natasha Parry) and/or the Elliott/Olivier Cordelia (Anna Calder-Marshall), and with the respective Gonerils and Regans.

Which Cordelia has more regal bearing? Which Cordelia appears to have the qualities needed to become queen of France?

Which Cordelia, in your opinion, is most likely to be able to lead the French troops in battle later in the play?

The Duke of Albany does not seem to be a role that stars would line up to try out for. However, the part is not an easy one: Albany has the task of standing in the wings at the opening of the play as his wife Goneril shares the spotlight with Lear. He becomes a person of no consequence in the hall scene where Goneril offends Lear.

In the second half of the play he must change from the "cowish" (IV, ii, 12), "milk-livered man" (IV, ii, 50) described by Goneril to the decisive regent in the final act. With a minimum of lines to develop his role, he must establish the character who gives commands, restores order, and, ultimately, sets the ship of state back on course.

Cutaway 13 Take 13

What does Albany, the "wallflower" in the first half of the play, do to prepare us for the regent who emerges in the final scenes of the play?

The three actors cast to play the difficult role of Albany (Arnold Moss in Brook/ Welles, Cyril Cusack in Brook/Schofield, and Robert Lang in Elliott/ Olivier) each presents a different persona for Albany in the first half of the play.

Cutaway 13 Take 14

Using two or more of the available film translations, compare the presentation of Albany (bearing, attire, voice, strength of his language, reactions of other characters to him) in the throne room scene (I, i) and the palace hall scene (I, iv).

Early in IV, ii, Shakespeare's Albany becomes forceful in his berating of his wife: "O Goneril, You are not worth the dust which the rude wind/Blows in your face" (35-37), "Wisdom and goodness to the vile seem vile" (38), and "See thyself, devil!" (59). As O'Brien (1982) points out, in this scene Albany recognizes and rejects evil, a stark contrast to the vulgarity of Goneril and Regan.

Cutaway 13 Take 15

Which Albany seems to be the more believable future leader of an army and king of the country? Which actor, in your opinion, makes the most convincing conversion from wimp to master?

It is worth making similar comparisons of the actors who play the Fool and the Duke of Cornwall. Rosenberg characterized Alan Badel's performance as the Fool (Brook/Welles) as "a restless acrobat who tried ineffectively to talk as he bounced" (Rothwell and Melzer, 132).

Cutaway 13 Take 16

Contrast Badel's performance with that of Jack MacGowran (Brook/ Schofield) and John Hurt (Elliott/Olivier). Which Fool is most likely to keep the king's favour while poking fun at his follies? Which Fool seems most likely to be out of reach when the king's whip falls?

Complicating the King

While the goodness of Cordelia and Kent or the evil of Goneril and Regan might limit the latitude of the performers in these roles, the complexities of the role of Lear invite a variety of performances and interpretations.

It has been argued that there is a certain playfulness and humanity in Olivier's performance that is lacking in those of Welles and Schofield. Collecting evidence to discuss this argument requires a careful examination of Olivier's entrance: what atmosphere is created by his holding onto Cordelia and apparently joking with her as he enters the throne room? As serious film readers, we might also focus on his kidding with Regan as she prepares to tell him how much she loves him and contrast this with his stern demand—only moments earlier—that Goneril kiss the rug. Olivier's facial expression in this scene is particularly noteworthy as we consider the effect of using the camera to focus on an apparent twinkle in his eye, and observe the playfulness (or is it mean teasing?) when he appears to invite Regan to kiss his ring. If these initial glimpses of Olivier's Lear are described as playful and warm, what words could be used to describe the initial Lear of Welles or Schofield?

Cutaway 13 Take 17

The range of talents required of actors performing the role of Lear is illustrated in three specific scenes: the hall scene at the Duke of Albany's palace (I, iv); the heath scene (III, ii); and the final scene (V, iii). Choose one of these scenes and compare the performances of at least two actors. Which actor appears to have captured the state of Lear's mind best in this scene? Use such criteria as voice, facial expression, bearing, empathy, sincerity, believability, and presence to decide which Lear is the more effective.

Major Productions

Rothwell and Melzer (1990) list forty-four versions and adaptations of *King Lear* which fall into four general categories:

- full length movie productions with sets;
- films or videotapes of stage versions;
- educational productions—generally short films designed to explore a particular scene or theme—whose purpose is to instruct rather than to entertain; and
- adaptations, derivatives, spoofs, or productions exploring parallel themes.

Four full-length productions and four adaptations/parodies are described below.

Four versions of *King Lear* produced over forty-five years take different production slants and offer interesting opportunities for comparison.

- *King Lear* (1953). Because it was co-directed by Peter Brook who also directed a full length production in 1969 and because it stars Orson Welles, this short (73–minute) film elicits more interest than it otherwise would. The major shortcoming of this version is that it cuts entirely the subplot of the evil illegitimate son Edmund, the part of the play Shakespeare adapted from Sidney's *Arcadia*. As noted above, this causes several problems with the audience's preparation for the final fight between Edgar and Edmund.

- *King Lear* (1969). Director: Peter Brook; Lear: Paul Schofield. In Brook's words, he presented "Shakespeare's rough, uneven, jagged, and disconcerting vision" (Rothwell and Melzer, 135). Schofield's Lear is frequently cited as "one more sinning than sinn'd against," citing Proudfoot's response. Although Shakespearean scholar Frank Kermode felt that this production was very good and underrated, a more common view was that held by Pauline Kael: "Peter Brook's *King Lear* is grey and cold, and the actors have dead eyes. I didn't just dislike this production; I hated it. . . . The conception is resolutely joyless and unbeautiful—a 'Lear' without passion, 'Lear' set in a glacial desert" (Rothwell and Melzer, 135).

- *King Lear* (1982). Director: Jonathan Miller; Lear: Michael Horden. From the BBC series "The Shakespeare Plays," this film was designed for television viewers. Horden won critical acclaim for his performance, his interpretation of Lear being a bumbler rather than a tyrant.

- *King Lear* (1984). Director: Michael Elliot; Lear: Sir Lawrence Olivier. This production was generally well received and critics praised it both for its vision of Lear (focussing on his suffering and his conversion) and for its overall effect: Rothwell and Melzer describe this version as a "symphonic poem" similar to Franz Liszt's Dante.

Adaptations, Derivatives, and Parodies

When directors choose the screen rather than the stage as the medium for Shakespearean plays, the productions are still quite obviously Shakespearean: the plot, the language, the script are all very similar to those watched by Shakespeare's audiences.

However, when film-makers are intrigued with the themes of the plays rather than the scripts, seeing the connection between the adaptation and the original play is not always easy. Five films outlined below were made for general audiences, so the debt to Shakespeare may or may not be obvious. Consider the value of films like these to increase our appreciation and understanding of the play-text.

- *Ran* (1985). In this Japanese adaptation of *King Lear*, three sons of a medieval Japanese warlord, Hidetora, feud over the power that their ageing father can no longer exercise. Hidetora bestows his authority but not his royal titles on his eldest son, Taro, but his other two sons object and the youngest is banished for his insolence. However, the evil in the movie is vested in Taro's wife, Lady Kaede, not the children. A documentary *The Making of Ran* is also available (see Rothwell and Melzer, 144). Although it can be found on public television from time to time, *Ran* is not generally recommended for viewing in secondary schools because of its length; however, students may find it extremely interesting to identify the cultural differences which are responsible for the adaptations in the Japanese version.
- *Lear* (1987). In this derivative/spoof of *King Lear*, Pulitzer Prize-winning author Norman Mailer revises the play as an allegory for the struggle for power in the modern-day Mafia. Added to the mix is Shakespeare's great-great-great (thirteen times) grandson who feels destined to film a late-twentieth century production of *King Lear.* The all-star cast (Peter Sellers, Burgess Meredith, Molly Ringwald, and Woody Allen) might predict a strong production, but the critics either panned or ignored it and it is now usually seen only on late night television.
- *A Thousand Acres* (1997) is set in the American Midwest. The film is a screen development of Jane Smiley's novel. Michelle Pfeiffer and Jason Robards struggle to suggest that the inheritance of the farm is as important as that of a kingdom. Scriptwriter Laura Jones and director Jocelyn Moorhouse appear to have had little say in the final Hollywood cut. Some argue that Shakespeare's themes are timeless; this film is a good reason to read the novel.
- *The Dresser* (1985). On one level, this is a play about the relationship between a star and his valet, but on other levels, it is indebted to Shakespeare. First, Albert Finney, the star of a troupe of travelling Shakespearean actors in Great Britain, performs scenes from *King Lear* as an actor, a central part of the movie. However, the backstage look at the troupe sug-

gests parallels with Lear: "Sir," the over-the-hill Shakespearean actor is a real-life "Lear" while his "Dresser" Norman plays the part of the fool.

- *Broken Lance* (1954). Although *Broken Lance* is frequently cited as a derivative of *King Lear*, the connection is somewhat tenuous. The protagonist of the movie, Mat Devereux, has four sons, three of whom are disloyal (their inclinations are similar to those of the children of both Lear and Gloucester). Like Lear, Devereux is out of touch with the times. Both Spencer Tracy (Devereux) and E.G. Marshall were stars at the time the film was made, but three of Tracy's stage sons—Robert Wagner, Richard Widmark, and Hugh O'Brian—went on to become stars in their own rights.

Closure

CHAPTER FOURTEEN

But What Happened in the End?

When events happen out of sequence, or do not logically follow each other, or result in an illogical ending, we find the film disjointed and difficult to follow. In extreme cases we might leave the theatre before the end of the film. When the film ends without providing an acceptable ending then we become very aware of our need for loose ends to be tied up, for closure. Polanski shows Macbeth "struck withal" by the predictions of the three witches but he closes the film with Donalbain visiting the witches' cave. The ending suggests that Shakespeare's play will be repeated over and over again, that it is timeless. In our desire for closure we can accept this idea, though it is not written in any of the play-texts we have for the play.

The demand for closure is also used to decide whether characters and events are believable. When Petruchio arrives late for his wedding with Katherine (in *The Taming of the Shrew*), we are not surprised because we have been shown his character. We expect him to do something unusual, even bizarre, and we are not disappointed by his lateness or by the strangeness of his costume when he arrives. We are certainly not surprised at Katherine's outrage when he arrives.

The same closure demand also allows us to accept that the shrew, Katherine, may have come to love Petruchio but we expect her to maintain a strong, individual identity. Shakespeare's play-text supports a range of film interpretations which can all suit our demand for a realistic logic.

Shakespeare, Spielberg, and Sequels

Modern film-making involve such vast financial outlays that film-makers are continuously seeking ways to increase box office return on their initial capital outlay. As a result, we have seen an increase in merchandising and a conscious effort to see film soundtracks, in particular, as separate commercial products.

A further development in late twentieth century film-making is the tendency to create ambiguous endings where closure is incomplete. The result is the potential for a sequel, a follow-up film that draws on the popularity of the original to sell itself at the box office. Spielberg has been claimed in some quarters as a modern-day Shakespeare because of both the diversity and the success of his film-making ventures. His approach differs from Shakespeare's, however, in that he often establishes the potential for a sequel to his films by deliberately leaving certain elements unresolved that can be picked up in future films.

More obvious sequels, like *Rambo* 2, 3, . . . , *Terminator* 25, 26, . . . , and all of the *Son of* . . . adventures, provide their sequel potential while achieving satisfactory closure by completing an adventure while leaving their central character alive to "fight another day."

Shakespeare, presenting probably only two "new" plays each summer, needed to create a sense of "newness" about every play. Some characters, like Sir Toby Belch, were very popular with audiences and they appeared in several different plays. More frequently, however, the need for closure required a strong resolution of all major themes and a sense of completion for the intentions of all major characters. The number of deaths at the close of *Hamlet* suggests one method of achieving this level of closure.

Hamlet

All performances of Shakespeare involve the translation of available play-scripts into performance by live actors. As such, they demand both a reading and a construction of the text. As directors make decisions about staging, costume, and setting, they have already begun the process of translation. They may do so in conventional ways, presenting a play in accordance with traditions established over four hundred years of its existence, or they may embark on more radical departures, taking account of contemporary concerns or of whatever else seems most relevant to their producers. The performances of the actors are similarly influenced. All may interpret their characters in a unique way, according to personal or directorial insights; each, however, must read that character in relation to the characters they are playing opposite.

The finished production may choose to emphasize a particular theme at the expense of others. Social violence, incest, arranged marriage, corruption in business are only a few possibilities. Hence a given production may also show a completely different play from that made available in another production. The business of reading a film is always affected by the text presented.

The production choices made by Laurence Olivier (1948), Franco Zeffirelli (1991), and Kenneth Branagh (1996) in their very different presentations of *Hamlet* dramatically illustrate the effects of both reading and constructedness. The much more obscure version from Finland, *Hamlet Goes Business*, directed by Aki Kaurismäki, modernizes the play while placing it in the business world in a way similar to the British TV adaptation of *Julius Caesar* (*Heil Caesar*).

Cutaway 15 Take 1

Compare the openings of the Olivier, Zeffirelli, and Branagh (four-hour version) *Hamlet*s. How does each set the tone for what is to follow? What cinematic techniques are most evident and why have they been chosen?

The Domestic Prince

Olivier is very explicit about how he wants his film to be viewed. A voice-over in the opening sequences informs us that "This is the tragedy of a man who could not make up his mind." We first meet a brooding Hamlet, seated a good deal of the time while giving vent to his bitterness about his mother's hasty and incestuous marriage to his uncle within two months of his father's death. A number of the key soliloquies are delivered as voice-overs with Hamlet seated, apparently unsure what to do for the best.

Cutaway 15 Take 2

Hamlet's soliloquies are among the most famous sections of the play. Examine one of them, for example, "To be or not to be," as performed by Olivier, Gibson, and Branagh. Which do you admire most from the point of view of an actor's performance? Which do you feel contributes most to a perceptive reading of the play?

Olivier stresses a strongly Oedipal relationship between Hamlet and his mother. Critics have noted the view of Gertrude's empty bed in the opening sequences as being suggestive of a woman's vagina. The bed is prominent in the arras scene when Hamlet kills Polonius. Part of Hamlet's struggle with his mother takes place in and around this same bed. Olivier was forty at the time of the filming and Eileen Herlie, who plays Gertrude, was twenty-seven, so it is probably not surprising that the scene has considerable sexual frisson—even when viewed almost half a century later. Zeffirelli's *Hamlet* with Mel Gibson and Glenn Close is even more explicit while Branagh's *Hamlet*, on the other hand, is not provided with any apparent sexual yearnings for his mother. What seem to be simple directorial choices provide us, as film readers, with a range of interpretative options. Their effectiveness becomes a challenge for us as readers and our judgment of the director's choice becomes an issue in our determining the effectiveness of the translation.

In the final act of the play when Hamlet is duelling with the treacherous Laertes, Olivier's Gertrude views the poisoned cup. A look of recognition on her face, she deliberately drinks from it, against the instructions of the king: "Gertrude, do not drink!" Having realized the extent of the king's plotting, Gertrude appears to sacrifice herself heroically to save her son. But is this a sustainable translation? It appears to rely on Hamlet's love for his mother being returned—even to the death, or is she so disgusted when she realizes the true deception of Claudius that she chooses death before a loveless marriage?

To form a reasoned assessment of this translation, it is useful to examine the play-script to see what has been cut and what, if anything, has been added.

What is "Not" in Olivier's Hamlet

Rosencrantz and Guildenstern disappear, as does Fortinbras. The political dimension at both courtly and national levels is also removed. We are given a *Hamlet* that dwells upon the prince's point of view and his personal dilemmas. Often the shots of what is happening reflect the world as he sees it. Despite its two-and-a-half hours, and in contrast to Parker's *Othello* for example, the film can seem to be rather slow-moving by contemporary standards. The camera's movement to different parts of the castle as the scene changes seems to reflect Hamlet's inactivity.

The omission of Hamlet's friends and acquaintances allows Olivier to establish a "domestic" *Hamlet* in which the deadly tussle between the prince, his uncle, and his mother predominate. This approach denies us a clear view of Hamlet's uncle, now his stepfather, Claudius. In the absence of any other information, we are forced to see Claudius through Hamlet's, possibly quite biased, eyes. Claudius's role as an elder statesman becomes obscured and the wisdom of his independent motivations is hard to read. To provide our-

 Key Shot Spoken alone on stage, the soliloquy usually tells us what the actor is thinking when action cannot reveal it and dialogue would be unsuitable for more private thoughts. The film voice-over is similar but need not be the same.

Establishing Shot 2
In a Greek tragedy by Sophocles, Oedipus killed his father and married his mother. The psychologist Sigmund Freud suggested that it was common for young boys to love their mother and, during early adolescence, even to have sexual feelings towards her. Freud called this the "Oedipus Complex" and recognized that it was a phase of development which was both normal and, in normally developing boys, relatively brief.

Translating the play-text of *Hamlet* is complicated because it exists in three significant variations, the First and Second Quartos, and the First Folio. Interestingly, Quarto 1 is usually regarded as a version constructed from the memories of actors by persons wishing to pirate the text; Quarto 2 appeared somewhat hastily in its wake, presumably to correct its errors. Folio 1 was published after Shakespeare's death. None of these texts can be regarded as canonical, that is, as Shakespeare's preferred version—if there ever was such a thing. Producers are free to make whatever use they will of all three play-scripts, and they do. Hence really radical differences can exist between performances of *Hamlet*, usually influenced by producers' and directors' readings of the play.

selves with a clearer view of Claudius's motivations, we are well advised to compare the written play-script with Olivier's film translation.

Hamlet as a Lethal Weapon

Zeffirelli's *Hamlet* is an interesting immediate comparison because in some respects it is clearly influenced by Olivier, while taking a contradictory approach to the prince. Domesticity prevails and the Oedipal relationship between Gertrude and Hamlet is even more obvious. The more then forty years between the two translations allows many on-camera sequences that Olivier could not have sneaked past the censors. Kisses and other demonstrations of physical affection exceed what we might expect between mother and son. The use of the bed is even more passionate. Though Gertrude does not knowingly drink the poison in Act V, Hamlet exchanges a knowing wink with her as he begins to fight Laertes. Is this to impress her with his manly fortitude?

What Zeffirelli does very differently, however, is to reverse Olivier's reading of *Hamlet*. It was not Mel Gibson's training as a classical actor in Australia that won him the title role, but rather, the impression he made on Zeffirelli as a man of action in *Lethal Weapon*. His Hamlet has more in common with Sylvester Stallone than with Olivier. He is constantly restless and we notice that many speeches are delivered to him and by him when he is on the move. It is as though he can hardly settle long enough to hear what is said to him. This does not preclude his lingering on a parapet to observe what is going on below or pausing to say farewell to his mother as he leaves for England (Zeffirelli's touch is not in the original play-text), but these add further to the sense of action.

Cutaway 15 Take 3

If you were a producer making a film of *Hamlet,* who would be your ideal choices of actors to play the main roles? Why would you choose these actors? In what ways would this combination of actors be effective in conveying your interpretation of the play?

Hamlet is seen as a man of indecision and inaction in the Olivier translation but in the Zeffirelli translation he seems, more often, to be deciding what he will do next. On board ship he substitutes different letters for the ones carried by the sleeping Rosencrantz and Guildenstern. He seems to have guessed the importance of the originals and as we see him reading them, we realize that he had planned the substitution before being certain of what was in the letters.

The inclusion of Rosencrantz and Guildenstern in the Zeffirelli production foregrounds an element of court intrigue which seems to have been deliberately reduced in Olivier's version. It also provides an international context in which Denmark is attached to a wider world. Most notably, however, it provides opportunities for the action hero to demonstrate his abilities. The scene where the two schoolfellows are beheaded becomes less symbolic of the political dependency of England on Denmark than it is of the hero's capacity to be one step ahead of his adversaries and, indeed, to "hoist" them on "their own petard." Significantly, there is still no sign of Fortinbras in this translation. Instead of opening with the play-script scene on the battlements, Zeffirelli begins with the funeral of old Hamlet to establish the positions of Hamlet, Claudius, and Gertrude.

Cutaway 15 Take 4

From Zeffirelli's funeral scene alone, identify the relationships between Hamlet and Gertrude; Hamlet and Claudius; and Gertrude and Claudius Explain how these relationships are constructed by the use of camera angle and lighting. Suggest why Zeffirelli might choose to establish the major characters before he introduces the basis for the story line.

Zeffirelli interpolates speeches and scenes to suit his purpose; for example, parts of Hamlet's nunnery speeches to Ophelia are transposed to a later time in the film-text than they are in the play-text. It seems that Zeffirelli is employing the possibilities of the film for greater fluidity than is feasible in a play, and highlighting speeches he wishes highlighted. In doing so, he is able to construct his own interpretation as an experienced and late-century filmmaker: "the Zeffirelli translation."

To Cut or Not to Cut

In Kenneth Branagh's film there is an enhanced sense of size and scope which is partly a result of his using the most complete compilation of play-scripts (and a consequent extra one-and-a-half hours of playing time).

Cutaway 15 Take 5

Kenneth Branagh filmed his *Hamlet* at Blenheim Palace in England and he dressed his characters in nineteenth-century costumes. Suggest why Branagh might have chosen an English rather than a Danish castle for his setting. Discuss the effect this information has on your response to the film.

Key Shot All productions of Shakespeare use edited and often abridged texts. Whole scenes, events, or characters may be left out—or added. Sometimes the action is rearranged. This is particularly necessary with a play like *Hamlet* which takes about four hours if played fully (as in the complete Branagh film version). Most productions are no more than three hours. The play-text prologue of *Romeo and Juliet* states that it will be two hours. Both the Olivier and Zeffirelli films are around two-and-a-half hours and each leaves out major sections of text.

The tone of the Branagh translation is set with the opening, focussing on the title, *Hamlet*. It becomes apparent that this name is carved at the base of the statue of the late King of Denmark. The statue stands before the imposing royal palace, vigilantly guarded by soldiers in the bleak winter landscape.

The statue embodies much that will be important in the story. It is a monument to a recently murdered man whose restless spirit is taking action to induce his son to avenge a wrong. This is the private and personal motivation that will affect young Hamlet. But that man was also a king and his regal importance is apparent when his brother and successor addresses the assembled court. The room is vast and splendid, the courtiers numerous, their dress costly and magnificent. We become aware that this translation is a big budget film with access to the most recent technology and an all-star cast. This knowledge will become part of our reading of the translation when we compare it with the earlier versions—particularly the Olivier translation.

Cutaway 15 Take 6

Since *Hamlet* is a long play, nearly all productions make considerable cuts to the text to reduce playing time to approximately two hours. Compare the Olivier, Zeffirelli, and Branagh (two-hour version) films of *Hamlet* to determine what sections of the play have been omitted. Consider why the cuts were made. Do they contribute to the success of the film? If you were a producer what sections would you consider essential to your translation? It has been argued that the greater length actually increases the dramatic tension and that Branagh's (four-hour) translation is the fastest paced of the three films. Is this a reasonable observation?

Claudius's first speech makes reference to the troubled relationship between Denmark and Fortinbras. The dead king was responsible for the death of Fortinbras's father and the king of Norway has had difficulty in restraining his nephew from taking retaliatory action. At various later points in the film there are cutaways to Fortinbras and his troops, ostensibly now merely seeking permission from Denmark to cross its soil to fight the "Polak."

At the end, while Hamlet and Laertes play out their final scene, Fortinbras's troops surround the palace, surprise and overcome the guards, and move into the building. As the members of the royal house of Denmark lie recently dead, soldiers crash through the glass doors on all sides while young Fortinbras enters triumphantly from below, somewhat bemused by the carnage that confronts him. He seizes the throne that moments before Hamlet has bequeathed him and is very gracious in his treatment of the body of the prince. Fortuitously, Fortinbras's transition to power is assisted, though it is unlikely that he would have been baulked by any opposition, and Horatio is left to explain the scene.

The film ends with the pomp of Hamlet's funeral and with Fortinbras's soldiers tearing down the statue of old Hamlet. Its head falls in front of the carved name. Unlike Hamlet and Laertes, Fortinbras's dead father is avenged with the fullest possible benefit to the avenger.

Intrigue in Court

Fortinbras can be seen as critically important in Branagh's translation because he helps us to see the complexity in Hamlet's view of himself as an avenger. Killing a king is no small task—as both Macbeth and Richard III discover—but killing a king in prayer or asleep may be even harder. Fortinbras has an army to assist him. Branagh's Hamlet is the deeply suspect son of the new king's predecessor. He can expect to be surrounded by the panderers, spies, and henchmen of his now-stepfather, Claudius. Polonius is the most prominent of these. Polonius can be shown as a prosy old fool but he is shown more importantly by Olivier and Zeffirelli to be single-minded in his scrutiny of Hamlet.

As readers of each translation, we are challenged to decide whether Polonius's interest in Hamlet is best related to his loyalty to his former king, his self-interest as Ophelia's father, or his determination as a political survivor to the new king, Claudius. In every case, Hamlet's "antic disposition" can be seen as a desperate device to take the heat off. Perhaps he hopes that if his actions seem deranged they will seem less threatening to the king, but the Claudius of Branagh's translation is too shrewd to let them pass and he plans to remove Hamlet, initially to England.

Cutaway 15 Take 8

View the scene between Hamlet and Ophelia spied upon by Polonius and Claudius in each of the three film translations. Discuss the major differences between the three scenes. What possible motivations does each version provide for Hamlet's apparent mistreatment of Ophelia? What other motivations can you suggest for his behaviour? Which of the three Hamlets do you find most acceptable in this scene?

Both Zeffirelli's and Branagh's Rosencrantz and Guildenstern are willing tools in Claudius's efforts to scrutinize Hamlet's motivations and control his behaviour. The prince's initial happiness in seeing his old school friends is quickly tempered when he perceives their real intent. For Branagh though, Claudius's court reflects a political reality which is extended to a national and even international level by young Fortinbras. It is a dangerous place where an insecure, newly installed monarch must be particularly alert to look after his royal person and his newly acquired position.

Gertrude's love for her son and his prominence as prince are helpful in Hamlet's struggle with his stepfather but they are not enough to protect him. Claudius, in every translation, is the ruthless and treacherous murderer of his brother. When matters become really desperate, Branagh's Claudius is quick to notice the same qualities in Laertes and pervert them for his final strike against Hamlet.

The Character of Claudius

In Branagh's four-hour film translation, it is significant that Claudius has a life of his own. He is not simply the incestuous husband of Hamlet's mother nor the lurking murderer that he appears to Hamlet in the other two films. We see more of him away from Hamlet than in the other two productions. As a result, we have more insight into his motivations. He is not just what Alfred Hitchcock called the "McGuffin" (the excuse for the action) but a substantial figure with his own aspirations and difficulties. He has to deal with the threats of both Hamlet, at home, and Fortinbras, beyond his immediate kingdom, while wishing to enjoy the love of the woman for whom he has sacrificed so much. As his attempt to pray, witnessed but not heard by Hamlet in Branagh's translation, shows, he is more complex than the arrant villain of previous productions.

Claudius knows what he has done and it appears to cause him conflict but he has opted for a worldly course and remains committed to his choice. He is careful in his selection of the instruments who will do his bidding and quick to assess what is afoot. The confrontation between Hamlet and Ophelia that Polonius sets up, and which he witnesses, is an effective ploy from his point of view in establishing just how dangerous the prince is.

Director's Cut 2

The fullness of Branagh's text allows us insights into Claudius that are denied in the heavily cut previous versions. Four hours of film opens up opportunities for background and character study that are usually only available to us as we read the play-scripts in their various versions—a difficult task for even the most dedicated scholars.

Working in small groups, consider how you would support an extended answer to the question: "Is it reasonable to compare the cinema translations of Olivier and Zeffirelli with the Branagh project of creating a film record of the complete play-script?"

Derek Jacobi's performance displays Claudius as a man of steely nerve with a self-control that underpins his regal dignity. Both qualities have been essential in getting him where he is. In each of the other films, Claudius reacts strongly to the scenario that Hamlet has set up to unmask him. He delivers the line "Give me some light! Away!" in the traditional manner—which seems to leave no doubt that he is shocked and distressed.

While it is equally clear that Jacobi's Claudius is affected, he speaks the line with visible control and contained emotion. He still provides Hamlet and Horatio with the confirmation needed to pursue the Ghost's injunction—but he has not been so easily caught out. Branagh's Claudius is a man whose past success has been achieved through his presence of mind. Because of their substantial shortening, earlier versions necessarily omit these subtleties.

Cutaway 15 Take 9

"The play-within-a-play used to trick Claudius into admitting his killing of the older Hamlet takes time to set up and this time slows the progress of the film. It would be better substituted with a different approach in a modern film version."

Working in small discussion groups, consider the effect of completely removing the play sequence from the Zeffirelli translation. What effect would this have on Hamlet's decision not to kill Claudius while he is praying? Would the removal of the play-within-a-play seriously affect Hamlet's motivation in the Olivier translation?

The Avengers: Hamlet and Fortinbras

In Branagh's full film translation, the morally compromising dimensions of the role of the avenger are confronted and interrogated. Hamlet's private vengeance must always have a public aspect. This is equally true for Fortinbras whose righting of the wrong done to his father is played out entirely in the public arena.

On the other hand, Laertes' response to the death of Polonius is motivated completely by personal grievance and leads to the unedifying spectacle of his rushing into the palace at the head of a group of thugs to attack the king. When he is finally appraised of the facts, his feelings are summed up in his willingness to cut Hamlet's "throat i' th' church!"—which seems to suggest that he is more ruthless than Hamlet, who had the opportunity to do this to Claudius.

While Laertes becomes a willing contributor to Claudius' plot against Hamlet, his innocent anger contrasts markedly with Hamlet's perception of the impossibility of his own position. He has previously had the opportunity to kill the king at prayer. This location intensifies Hamlet's dilemma about killing Claudius immediately as it recalls the irony of the king's concluding lines:

My words fly up, my thoughts remain below: Words without thoughts never to heaven go. (III, iii, 97–98)

It also renders more stark Hamlet's decision not to act because, if his killing the king were to result in Claudius going to heaven, this would not be revenge. The inactive, frequently seated Hamlet of Olivier's translation can be justified on this point. Hamlet is mindful, of course, that his own father was unshriven and the punishment would not fit the crime. But more starkly, it puts Hamlet into the position of the avenger who must lower himself to the moral level of his victim. It is this moral awareness that makes it so hard for Hamlet to embrace his task, adds to his anguish and generates what the Elizabethan audience would clearly see as a tragic dilemma. Yet it is not merely the Ghost's imperative that impels Hamlet to revenge but also his political position. Neither of Branagh's Fortinbras nor Laertes has any trouble with either. Laertes, his father's son, shows little apparent concern for the moral/religious dilemma. Fortinbras sees beyond revenge to an expanded kingdom. Each willingly embraces a part in the corruption he purportedly opposes. Zeffirelli's "Hamlet-as-Lethal Weapon" does not linger in this dilemma. As a man of action he moves on quickly.

Cutaway 15 Take 10

"Laertes is a minor character with a major role for both Olivier and Zeffirelli." Is this complaint equally true for the four-hour Branagh film?

Hamlet the Lover

Kenneth Branagh's playing of Hamlet reinforces the sense of a man beset with an impossible dilemma. It is not that he is a man who cannot make up his mind, but that he cannot be sure what action is appropriate. He is a restless and active figure, fully aware of the dangers of his position and resenting them, quick to sum up the motivations of others, trusting only in Horatio. A poignant example is in his dealings with Ophelia. His love is established in shots of him in bed with her, tenderness a key note in what we are shown. He is at first gentle with her when he meets her in the mirrored hall but as he realiszes that she is a willing tool of her father and the king who are spying on them through the glass of a double mirror, his fury knows no bounds. Like the presidents, politicians, and film stars of today, Hamlet cannot have a personal life in the same way that other people can. The prince's accuracy of perception is no help in solving his difficulties. He can, at every turn, sum up the situation but he cannot do anything about it. He is Zeffirelli's man of action controlled by Olivier's man who cannot make up his mind.

Translating and Editing

Each of the three films represents a distinctive translation of Shakespeare's *Hamlet*. Both the choice of text and its presentation are essential elements in our reading. Careful choices are made in the productions to focus attention and shape response. The film medium gives unique opportunities to highlight dramatic moments and to comment on the action. The constructedness of this process becomes clearer when the Olivier and Zeffirelli films are compared with the two-hour version made from Branagh's original. The Branagh version seems less satisfactory than the other two because it is barely half of the original from which it comes. Huge chunks, such as the opening battlement scenes, most of the scenes involving the players, and, crucially, the scene of Claudius at prayer, are omitted.

Dissatisfaction for the viewer may come from a close knowledge of the play-script or the uncut four-hour film but it is difficult to remove the impression of a series of excerpts rather than a satisfactory whole. The two-hour version was not conceived as a whole and many of the links and bridges between scenes that could have been made are missing. In contrast, Olivier and Zeffirelli also omit large chunks of the original and remould the characters and their places in the resulting plot to create a new translation. A viewer may or may not be impressed with the result but is more likely to accept its coherence. Inevitably, the play we receive through the film is not only the Bard's but someone else's as well. The film is an experience, not of Shakespeare's *Hamlet*, but of Olivier's or Zeffirelli's or Branagh's.

Translation and Cultural Context

Translation must necessarily accept the cultural context into which it is read. Olivier's *Hamlet* was released shortly after the conclusion of the World War II. Its success owes much to its audience being able to recognize the survival of the smaller power against overwhelming odds. Zeffirelli's translation followed much lesser engagements such as the Falklands War. His man-of-action has to go out into an unjust world seeking vengeance. Branagh's *Hamlet* followed the first media war, the "Desert Storm" of the Gulf War with Iraq. Having developed the totality of a film translation in four hours, the cut in which Branagh halves the film length must inevitably remove key motivations, links, and even events. Like the media production of the Gulf War—reported every evening on the 6 pm television news—and the confused reporting of the actions of Serbs, Croats, Albanians, and Moslems in the former Yugoslavia, Branagh's two-hour *Hamlet* leaves us slightly dissatisfied. Have we really understood the action? Do we really know why it is happening? Do we even understand who the key players are—or what they really stand for?

Cutaway 15 Take 13

One of the conventional reasons for continuing to study Shakespeare's plays is that their themes are timeless. Using historical examples from local, national, and international politics, consider the role of family relationships in causing social unrest or upheaval. How important are family relationships in establishing later individual actions in the wider society? What places do revenge and jealousy have in national and international politics?

Further Possibilities for Discussion

1. Compare the scene involving Hamlet, Polonius, and Gertrude in her bedroom as it is shown by Olivier, Zeffirelli, and Branagh. What do you learn from this scene about (a) the translation of *Hamlet* given in the film, and (b) the relationships of the three characters in the play as a whole?

2. Olivier plays Hamlet as a man of inaction; Gibson plays him as a man of action; Branagh plays him as a sensitive man enmeshed in a world of political intrigue. How is it possible for such widely variant renderings of the same character to appear on film? Is it reasonable to claim that any one of these performances is more authentically Shakespearean than the others? Establish detailed reasons for your view.

3. What advantages does a good film of *Hamlet* offer compared to a stage production? Are there any disadvantages?

4. In a film, pieces of "business" not in the original play-text can be crucial to the view of the play the audience is being given. Examine some examples of such business in any of the films of *Hamlet* you have seen. How do they contribute to the director's interpretation of the play?

5. Zeffirelli's *Hamlet* is medieval in appearance; Olivier's is roughly contemporary with Shakespeare. Branagh places the film in a more recent period. In what ways are our responses to the film guided by these settings?

6. Does Olivier's *Hamlet* gain or lose by being in black and white?

CHAPTER SIXTEEN

Romeo and Juliet

Acknowledging the Source

While scholars continue to discuss the authorship of Shakespeare's plays, it is clear that each was actually presented by Shakespeare's company of actors—though possibly never in the form we now have as the published play-script. It is generally accepted that the plays were probably never written down in their entirety while they were being performed, that they changed according to who was playing particular roles, and that they changed according to audience response and identity.

Documentary evidence suggests that *Romeo and Juliet* was probably developed as a play by Shakespeare's company in 1594 or 1595. Like many Elizabethan plays, it is based on stories popular at the time and known to the intended audience. Being set in Italy, it cannot be said to be talking about current events in England and its location, for the audience, is both exotic and, at the time, popular.

In his title sequence, Zeffirelli acknowledges the play as his production of William Shakespeare's *Romeo and Juliet*. Luhrmann takes this acknowledgment one step further and titles his film *William Shakespeare's Romeo and Juliet*. The acceptance by each director that he is working with material first developed by another author provides him with an excuse for modifying the script but suggests that each has a clear understanding of the text he is working from.

Zeffirelli's setting of *Romeo and Juliet* in Verona accepts the historical and geographic locations provided by the play-text. As a result, we expect Shakespearean language and, where it is not made redundant by visual access to costume, properties, and scenery, Elizabethan manners and conventions. In stark contrast, Luhrmann has reinterpreted both time and place while maintaining the language of the play-text. The resulting film provides us with access to modern day characters speaking in a rather strange dialect of English. For some viewers this tends to create a tension between audience and production that forces a concentration on listening for meaning rather than watching for action. The effect is similar to viewing an Australian film in Canada or vice versa.

Establishing Shot 1

Numerous attempts have been made to film *Romeo and Juliet*. Only four have been considered as serious film interpretations of the play. The most acceptable to teachers and, later, to scholars, has been the 1968 Zeffirelli version which gained critical acclaim for its use of sixteen- and seventeen-year-old actors to play the title roles. In sharp contrast, the 1929 version directed by George Cukor starred Leslie Howard and Norma Shearer (both established and popular film stars but forty-three and thirty-six respectively at the time of filming—rather difficult to accept as teenagers). The 1954 version directed by Renato Castellani starred Lawrence Harvey (aged twenty-six) and Susan Shantall (aged twenty, in her only film). The most immediately popular film translation has been the recent 1996 Luhrmann version which quickly captured the imagination of teenaged audiences, many of whom have seen this film multiple times without urging. This chapter will focus on the reading of particular sections and thematic issues from the readily available treatments of Baz Luhrmann and Franco Zeffirelli.

Director's Cut 1 It has been argued that because Luhrmann's film *William Shakespeare's Romeo and Juliet* requires close listening to the language and is presented in modern dress in a contemporary setting, it is a more accurate production of Shakespeare's intention than Zeffirelli's. Using your research into the way Elizabethan theatre was used as an entertainment, consider the validity of this argument.

Film as a Product of its Historical Setting

In the late 1960s, major media concerns revolved around the continuing battles between teenaged gangs in Britain and the increase in draft dodging and anti-Vietnam involvement in America. The musical impact of the Beatles on teen culture equalled the impact of the protest songs of Bob Dylan. The American National Guard had shot students protesting on campuses at Kent State in Ohio and at Berkeley in California. The president of the United States, John Kennedy, had been assassinated and so had the African-American civil rights leader, Martin Luther King, Jr. Parental guidance of children and challenges to traditional family values of obedience and subservience had come into question following widespread acceptance of a book on parenting by Dr. Benjamin Spock.

When Zeffirelli directed *Romeo and Juliet*, the rights of church and state were in question from the generation born after World War II. The age when childhood became adulthood was in serious dispute from young people likely to be conscripted to fight a war they did not understand on behalf of leaders they were unwilling to trust. The issues and themes which underlie the core of *Romeo and Juliet* were the focus of this generation.

Two generations later, and shortly after the Gulf War (which is widely accepted as the first war ever completely stage-managed for the media), Luhrmann directed a media-focussed version of the same play. Again, many of the major concerns of the media had been focussed around family values and authority appearing to have been rejected by the younger generation. Historically responsive to the times, Luhrmann's interpretation is set within a decaying social structure where appearance is more important than substance, drug-dependent teenaged gangs apparently hold the streets to ransom, sexuality is at least ambiguous in the face of the AIDS epidemic, and the simple values of love and forgiveness seem, again, to have been lost forever.

It has been argued that "the film version of a play can only reflect the values established within the play." *Romeo and Juliet* appears to be a play which can reflect its values through any place and any period. To what extent is any film interpretation of a play a construction of its director and screenwriters?

Opening the Film

Despite their vastly different approaches to film-making and to their interpretation of the play-script, both Zeffirelli and Luhrmann open their films with the prologue from the original play as a voice-over.

The Prologue [enter Chorus]
Chorus
Two households, both alike in dignity,
In fair Verona, where we lay our scene,
From ancient grudge break to new mutiny,
Where civil blood makes civil hands unclean.
From forth the fatal loins of these two foes
A pair of star-cross'd lovers take their life;
Whose misadventur'd piteous overthrows
Do with their death bury their parents' strife.
The fearful passage of their death-mark'd love,
And the continuance of their parents' rage
Which, but their children's end, naught could remove,
Is now the two hours' traffick of our stage;
The which if you with patient ears attend,
What here shall miss, our toil shall strive to mend.

[exit]

Zeffirelli's camera pans slowly from fog and smog across the outline of Verona beneath a weak and wintry sun before it zooms in to the town square. Luhrmann zooms slowly in to a television set on which a Hispanic female newscaster is broadcasting details of the latest street riots in a more modern but depressed, and apparently American, Verona Beach. As Luhrmann cuts to street scenes, viewers familiar with the play become quickly aware that billboards and hoardings carry quotes from the play-text.

Luhrmann's camera watches the opening scene unfold from above and afar—even clinically. As events unfold, we are close enough to note the detail but we remain far away enough to feel protected from the violence of the action. We see the guns, the looks on faces, the detail around the doorways, and in the advertising signs. It is familiar but not identical with our own environment. We anticipate the flames which end the scene and maybe even hope that the police will intervene.

In contrast, Zeffirelli takes his camera down into the square, among the stalls and between the feet of the vendors and buyers. As a result, we look up to the Capulets and the Montagues from our first viewing. We note their contrasting colours, their swaggering walks. As intimates in the marketplace, we are involved in the action, the insult, and the ensuing scuffle. We retreat with the camera as the Prince and his guard arrive. We are among the "enemies of peace" and we feel the threat that our "lives shall pay the forfeit of the peace."

Casting the Title Roles

In settings owing more to opera and ballet than Shakespeare's play-text, Zeffirelli presents an almost unbelievably romantic Romeo (Leonard Whiting) and a childishly naive Juliet (Olivia Hussey). The introduction of Romeo with soulfully darkened eyes and flowers in hand borrows heavily on the black-and-white make-up style of romantic film stars from the 1920s such as Rudolph Valentino or Mary Pickford. To teenaged audiences in the late 1990s, it makes Romeo an unlikely leader among the young Montagues, and suggests that Juliet would be too innocent to fall in love at first sight.

Unlikely as the romance seems, however, Zeffirelli effectively distances the world of romance from the harsh reality of civil strife. The result allows for meaningful observation of Juliet's family at home and some significant identification of the problems associated with arranged marriage. In contrast, it provides for a similar exploration of the depth of the family feuding. Luhrmann's version, filmed in Mexico, is most obviously a product of the media generation. The frenetic street violence of the large city is watched over by a gigantic statue of Christ, its arms outstretched, while the helicopters of law enforcement transcend even the power of the Church by buzzing around it like angry insects.

Like Zeffirelli, Luhrmann casts for youth though both Romeo (Leonardo di Caprio) and Juliet (Clare Dane) are somewhat more worldly-wise and possibly more credible in their context than Zeffirelli's "star-cross'd lovers." The consequence of this choice is a loss of family intimacy in the Capulet household. Luhrmann's Lady Capulet has more in common with an image-infatuated social-climbing shrew than with the embittered mother of seven dead children who thinks that her only surviving child is to be wed on her husband's orders at age fourteen.

The Arranged Marriage

Zeffirelli casts Juliet's suitor, Paris, as an old man—perhaps sixty, possibly even older. The potential mismatch with the thirteen-year-old Juliet is stark, even horrifying, in many western societies. Capulet's warning that there is much grief in marrying too young is highlighted as the camera looks over his shoulder to his embittered wife. Her age is uncertain but she also was married young, as Capulet tells Paris, and has been married at least fourteen years. She could be as young as twenty-seven, probably not older than thirty-eight. Capulet is at least sixty so Paris is relatively even older in seeking marriage with Juliet. We never know whether he has been married before—his wife/wives may have died in childbirth.

As Luhrmann focusses on the media opportunities flowing from the family feud, he creates a frenetic world of fast-cut editing where law enforcement is more threatening than family traditions and where the playboy Paris, Verona Beach's "most eligible bachelor of the year," is unlikely to be arranging to wed a thirteen-year-old. The brief discussion between Paris and Capulet adds little to our understanding of the unfolding events though it provides a showcase for Lady Capulet's socialite hysteria while debasing the role of the nurse in Juliet's upbringing.

Masque

On a dramatic level, the Capulet's masked ball is a simple device for allowing Romeo to meet Juliet. From an entertainment perspective, it probably provided the original Elizabethan audience with an opportunity to watch an equivalent of "Lives of the Rich and Famous." Its lengthy prologue sequence, where Mercutio makes fun of Romeo as a dreamer, allows Luhrmann to extend his use of mood-enhancing drugs as a method of reducing inhibition. The introduction of drugs is consistent with Luhrmann's interpretation of the play but the introduction of the Queen Mab story to explain dreams and dreamers seems irrelevant in this context.

Romeo's cat mask in the Luhrmann film can be seen in a number of ways but when Tybalt describes himself as the "King of Cats," the antagonism between the two families is refocussed. Tybalt sees Romeo at the ball and tells his father to have the Montagues removed. Capulet refuses and Tybalt's hatred is boundless. Through use of the masque, Luhrmann provides a stronger motivation for the later fight than Zeffirelli—though both tend to use it as a musical interlude from the violence. The families can, in fact, co-exist within the formalities of a clear social framework—which the prince has given them. More significantly, with or without masks, if the family name tags are removed, Romeo and Juliet can fall in love like any young people.

The Theatre of War

The "play within a play" structure which is commonly used to allow parallel actions to develop is not a feature of the play-text of *Romeo and Juliet*. However, the need to separate the reality of the family feud from the romance of the title characters requires a recognition of the differences between reality and fantasy.

Mercutio's cross-dressed performance as a nightclub entertainer blurs the lines defining sexuality in Luhrmann's film. Romeo's actions, his speech, his manner and, in Zeffirelli's version, his make-up and flower-carrying each suggest that he is more comfortable with his masculinity than with the male role he is expected to play.

Luhrmann's headquarters for the Montague gang, the stage of a wrecked theatre, is defined by the remaining proscenium arch. The auditorium has been demolished, there is no shelter, the projection box has gone, and the screen itself has been removed. Instead of a filmic fantasy, the gang sees reality—almost always stormy and usually at sunset. Ultimately, both Tybalt and Mercutio fall from the stage. Tybalt falls through the screen area, out of the theatre. Mercutio dies in the auditorium area, in the theatre of war.

Zeffirelli's approach, in some ways, is even more bleak. Neither gang is located in a stable environment. They meet together in the streets, they play on the steps of the church and at the well, but never enter any of the buildings. They climb narrow lanes and pass through arches but only Tybalt is ever at home (during the masque). Even then his home is invaded and he is helpless to respond.

Cutaway 16 Take 6

Luhrmann's film seems to provide or suggest many places for the gangs to meet. Zeffirelli's film seems too neat to allow a space. Sometimes it seems too clean and orderly for the tragedy to develop.

Use your research findings to design areas which could have been used by Zeffirelli to create spaces for the gangs to meet among themselves. Develop your findings as set drawings and models.

The Play as Social Commentary and Satire

It is usual to describe *Romeo and Juliet* as a tragedy resulting from a family feud. The prologue states that the play lasts for two hours, that it will show the deaths of two young people who fell in love, and that their families would not stop feuding until their deaths. More importantly, perhaps, the prologue asks the audience to listen carefully and promises that what they do not understand from hearing, they will be able to see in the action on stage.

The tone of the prologue suggests that the play will present a lesson to the audience. It seems unlikely, however, that an Elizabethan audience would walk to the theatre to stand watching an entertainment for two hours, possibly in the rain, if they were to be the target for a lesson in family politics. The play would be expected to present more conscious entertainment so it is worth considering alternative interpretations.

The relationship between the Catholic Queen Mary (known as "Bloody Mary"; queen 1553–1558) and her Protestant sister, Queen Elizabeth I (1558–1603), forms an historical background for the play so the Capulets and Montagues might represent the "families" of Catholic and Protestant believers. This interpretation would be dangerous for Shakespeare and his company if either group objected to the portrayal.

A number of playwrights were imprisoned for treason—some for long terms—because they hinted at criticism of the crown, the state, or the church in their works. This law was not rescinded until the 1970s!

The prologue states from its first line that the two households are "both alike in dignity." To be safe, however, the play concentrates its attention on the children of the families rather than their parents. In doing so, it allows the adults to avoid criticism. Adults, when they are able to distance themselves from the action, usually accept that young people may show their ignorance, engage in silly actions, and over-react to adult emotions. The action in *Romeo and Juliet* can be seen as a satire on children growing up. Even more importantly, as is usual in Shakespeare's plays, it can be seen as a satire on the actions and excesses of the "rich and shameless," the nobility, people in power in far away places—this time, in Italy.

In satirizing the adolescent children of the nobility, Shakespeare provides a platform from which to explore serious issues of parenting together with serious issues of government. Juliet's age is discussed by Paris and Capulet in relation to her child-bearing. Capulet dismisses her physical ability to bear children at age thirteen and considers, instead, the effect of multiple child-bearing and loss on the relationship between husband and wife. He suggests that Paris should wait at least until Juliet is sixteen. In different contexts—*The Taming of the Shrew* and *Merry Wives of Windsor*—similar discussions become the source of obvious humour. Zeffirelli foregrounds the theme of age readiness for marriage as he foregrounds the role of the nurse in mothering Juliet. The resulting scenes of farce provide a clear indication of the potential for satire within the play. Luhrmann, on the other hand, reduces these scenes to the point where the nurse becomes little more than a regularly abused messenger—first for Lady Capulet and then for Juliet.

The role of the church in assisting Juliet to marry Romeo remains difficult to interpret. It cannot be omitted because the pair need a "safe house" to meet in. Friar Lawrence is seen as an alchemist by both Zeffirelli and Luhrmann. Luhrmann is more pointed in suggesting that the priest is developing and distributing drugs and, furthermore, teaching the next generation (of choirboys) how to do likewise. He is presented as an ambiguous character, possibly wishing to help but apparently warped in his intention. Under his guidance, Romeo is presented as a spaced-out hero to the younger boys.

Fagan in *Oliver Twist* fills a similar role in saving Oliver from starvation but placing him in greater danger by training him as a thief—who will be imprisoned or even hanged if he is caught. In this parallel, Romeo appears to be the Artful Dodger.

Zeffirelli's friar is a slightly more innocent character, a well-intentioned creature of the night who tries to do the right thing for Juliet but mucks up. Either interpretation would suit Shakespeare's purpose in suggesting that the interference of the church in England was causing suffering to the "children of the church."

The events leading to the tragedy in which Juliet wakes to find that Romeo has committed suicide because he thought that she was already dead and so she commits suicide too, border on high farce. In both film interpretations, the camera succeeds in presenting compelling images but it remains among the weakest scenes. The deathbed speeches are powerful but they are the speeches of children who cannot understand that they have over-reacted to create their own tragedies. Zeffirelli allows the closing sequences to generate their own power and, for adult audiences, these are quite effective. Adolescent audiences are less forgiving and the high-camp ending of Luhrmann is more satisfying because it admits the farcical nature of the sequence. The church is more highly lit than for a coronation, the corpse of Juliet is effectively enthroned in virginal white and the finger-twitching of Juliet's "almost in time" recovery provides an acceptance of the melodrama which is confirmed when the camera cranes out to view the sanitized set-piece ending— the corpses carefully arranged across each other and a carefully arranged spattering of blood.

Further Possibilities for Discussion

1. It is a simple matter to suggest that both Romeo and Juliet died for their love of each other but this is a very unsatisfactory resolution to a more complex play. In fact, it is this interpretation which makes the play so difficult to present credibly. Romeo and Juliet have sought refuge in the church. They have been married in the church and their upbringing would have steeped them in the laws of the church. It is unlikely, under these circumstances, that suicide would have been seen as the immediate solution to their problems.

    Juliet deliberately, and under the guidance of her priest, fakes suicide to avoid marriage to a man she does not love—Paris. Luhrmann's film interpretation indicates that Romeo, already banished for his killing of Tybalt, accepts that his wife has committed suicide and therefore, grief-stricken, has nothing to lose by joining her. Zeffirelli does not make this link so clearly.

    When Juliet wakes to find that Romeo has taken his life from grief, she would appear to have several alternatives to suicide. Both Shakespeare and the film-makers, however, have already exhausted several of these.

    If Juliet had not faked suicide, she might have returned to her family, begged forgiveness, and married Paris. For both Zeffirelli and Luhrmann, this alternative has been eliminated in their decision to make an explicit scene of the consummation of the marriage.

    If Juliet had gone to the Montagues, told them she had married Romeo, and that the marriage had been consummated, she could beg their forgiveness and live with them. Unfortunately, Romeo's banishment and, more particularly, his suicide make this an impossible option because she is now the only living focus of the hatred between the families.

    If Juliet went away quietly, everyone could forget the tragic events and she could enter a nunnery.

    What other possibilities exist for saving Juliet from suicide? Suggest why both Shakespeare and the film-makers have accepted the multiple suicide ending although it goes against the teaching of the Roman Catholic church.

2. Music is used cleverly and constantly by both Zeffirelli and Luhrmann to extend the mood of the play and to develop relationships without the need for additional dialogue. The theme from Zeffirelli's *Romeo and Juliet* won an Oscar for Nino Rota. The central entertainment at Zeffirelli's

masque is the song that foreshadows the ending, "So dies the youth/So dies the fairest maid." Luhrmann portrays Mercutio as a nightclub entertainer and several of the sequences depend on his talent as an entertainer.

West Side Story presents an extreme example of the use of music by interpreting the play as a stage musical. The filmed version of the musical is readily available on videotape and provides a challenging extension of the concept of translation from one entertainment form to another.

Consider the use of music by each film-maker at critical points in the story. How does the different interpretation of each director provide him with options unavailable from the play-text?

3. Although several of the issues associated with the marriage of Romeo and Juliet can be equally discussed by reference to the play-text alone, reference to the filmed interpretations helps us towards a powerful understanding of:

- the role of the nurse in Juliet's upbringing—and in her death;
- the place of the arranged marriage in Elizabethan society and, in some modern societies at differing social levels.

Consider how the changing times during which the film translations of *Romeo and Juliet* have been completed have allowed their directors to extend the meaning of parenting available from the play-text.

4. *Romeo and Juliet* contains some of the best Elizabethan insults available from Shakespeare's play-texts. Identify the insults, discuss how they are supposed to work and consider whether the nature of the insult has been changed by each of the film-makers.

Gang warfare is presented quite differently by Zeffirelli and Luhrmann; the musical *West Side Story* provides a further alternative. Consider whether the social commentary on gang warfare is as important as the expression of tragedy for the lovers and suggest an alternative translation in which Romeo and Juliet become minor characters in the production. Suggest a name for your new film and identify the lead characters.

If Capulet had evicted the Montagues from the masque, Romeo would not have met Juliet and the tragedy could have been avoided. It is Capulet's treatment of Tybalt that moves the action from civil unrest to tragedy. Do you agree?

CHAPTER SEVENTEEN

Further Opportunities for Discussion

The Ensemble and Authorship

One of the assumptions behind the writing of much of this book is the belief that the actual writing of "Shakespeare's play-scripts" was never undertaken by Shakespeare. Instead, as the company owner and director, Shakespeare suggested the ideas and probably wrote major speeches which were needed to fit particular sections of each play. Using this belief, we can suggest that the reason for the folio and quarto versions of the Shakespeare plays was to record what people thought were memorable events so that they could be played again—much as we buy the videotape of a film or series so that we can watch it again at our leisure.

Like the audience for the Greek and Roman plays, the Elizabethan audience already knew most of the stories they were seeing on the stage. Like today's audiences, they were familiar with previous kings and queens, battles and romances. They were familiar with the probable intrigues and gossip that always surrounds famous people and, like modern audiences, they liked to see plays about what goes on between the rich and famous.

With this belief, it seems quite acceptable that every generation should remake its own translations of the Shakespeare plays in the medium that is most accessible and entertaining for them at the time. The theatre was the only available place to see organized entertainment until the invention of moving pictures. The cinema still required us to travel out of our homes to see the entertainment though, for the first time, the actors did not have to travel to the same theatre to present their entertainment. Television is the first medium which has allowed us to view organized entertainment in our own homes.

The value of considering Shakespeare's plays as the result of an ensemble of actors working together to develop an entertainment is that it allows us to see why different folios contain different texts, why there do not seem to be any remnants of Shakespeare's play-scripts written in his own hand, and why some of the lines could not have been delivered more than once in an Elizabethan theatre (consider the reference to a camel-shaped cloud in an open air theatre).

Establishing Shot 1

The recent film *Shakespeare in Love* presents a very amusing suggestion about how *Romeo and Juliet* came to be written and performed. Co-written by Tom Stoppard (who also wrote *Rosencrantz and Guildenstern Are Dead*, a derivative from *Hamlet*), the film provides excellent background about the life and times of young William Shakespeare. At the same time, it introduces Christopher Marlowe, Jon Webster, and a range of the essential names associated with Elizabethan theatre in a highly entertaining context.

Tom Stoppard, who provided the idea and co-wrote the screenplay for *Shakespeare in Love*, has been threatened with lawsuits for taking his ideas, and much of the action and dialogue, from an earlier play. The approach is truly Shakespearean. If it is a good play and a good idea then it should be seen and heard. Unfortunately, the concept of authorship is far more rigid in our own time than it was 300 years ago.

The role of the printing press has played a large part in hardening our ideas of who wrote what. Despite the work of editors and publishers in influencing writers to meet commercial demands or social expectations, the author of a printed work is considered to be a simply identifiable person or group of persons. The complexity of film-making, however, makes it difficult to attribute the authorship to any single member of the vast team who work on the production. Screenwriters, directors, producers, actors, and even sponsors may all shape the wording as much as the interpretation. Editors, similarly, create subtle differences which may create entirely different readings by sequencing shots to match the demands of music, sound, and dialogue.

Shakespeare in Love shows Christopher Marlowe giving Shakespeare an idea for a play, the leading actor agreeing to take a smaller part because it better fits the needs of the story, and accidental business on stage being included because it works. *Shakespeare in Love* provides some very useful possibilities for the interpretation and understanding of both Shakespearean playscripts and Elizabethan times.

Voice as Identity

Highly successful Hollywood actors have frequently had distinctive voices. Part of the benefit of a distinctive voice is that the public recognizes the actor from film to film. This may be seen as an aid to building star status. A second advantage of distinctive voices is that they help the audience keep the characters straight, especially in productions with large casts. Of course, there are other ways of helping the audience keep the characters straight: the use of similarly coloured costumes for the members of each clan (for example, the Montagues and the Capulets); and the liberal use of characters' names by other characters. List other methods that directors use to help audiences to remember who is who.

Some of the actors in these productions may be recognizable to you through their voices. Choose actors from the films whose voices you recognize from other films or television productions. List these actors and actresses and the other work they have appeared in. Working with others in a study group, create a poster which shows a picture of the actor and lists her or his film credits. Describe ways in which this actor's voice is distinct. Include a cassette tape of her or his voice from at least two other productions.

Make a list of famous movie actors who have distinctive voices. Include as many movies and roles as you can. Compare your list with those of others in your study group. Make a poster. Include a cassette tape with examples of their voices and see if others recognize the voices on tape.

Directors

Biographies of such famous directors as Alfred Hitchcock and Sir Laurence Olivier offer interesting insights into the visions of film directors and the ways they present them. Evan Hunter's *Me and Hitch* and Jon Tuska's *Encounters with Film-makers: Eight Career Studies* demonstrate the ways directors and producers contribute to the vision presented in films. Research the biographical details of the director of one of your favourite films. In a paragraph, outline the vision the director presents in the film. Cite evidence which shows either how the director came to this vision or which presents a similar or complementary vision. Write a review of the film describing the director's vision and introducing biographical data to support your position.

Cultural Capital

Parents and neighbours can be rich sources of folklore about characteristics associated with the birth order of children. Collect some of the lore surrounding birth order and compare it with information available from basic psychology books and parenting magazines. Is Goneril a typical oldest child? Is Cordelia a typical youngest? Pay particular attention to attributes of the middle child of three, Regan's position in her family. Discuss the likely response of a Shakespearean audience to Regan's actions during a performance of the play. Suggest how these reactions would affect a modern interpretation of Regan for a film production.

How important is it to have read the play-text before you can appreciate the film translation? What advantages are there in being familiar with the quotable quotes from a play before you watch the film translation?

Film Reviews/Book Reviews/Arts Reviews

Critics of the arts (drama, film, art, music, literature, etc.) can help readers, viewers, and audiences to understand and appreciate aesthetic works. Some people read the critics' opinions before deciding whether or not to attend or view or read a work. More often we read the critics following our experience of the work to compare their opinions with ours. Locate at least two reviews of one film translation of a recent Shakespearean play or movie and compare the reviewers' responses with your own. Write a review which presents and supports your opinions while acknowledging the opinions of the other reviewers.

Suicide

Despite being a Catholic in a Catholic country where suicide is a mortal sin, Juliet feels that she has no option but suicide because she has offended her own parents and married into a family who are sworn enemies. Othello does not seem to have any particular religious beliefs but takes his own life because he believes he has failed in his expectations of himself as a man.

Research the attitudes to suicide and to responsibilities between man and wife in Elizabethan society. Use your findings to suggest how Shakespeare was able to use suicide as a method of closing two of his tragedies.

Murder

Murder is used variously in Shakespeare's plays to provide motivations for revenge, to remove unwanted characters from the scene and to offer insights into the desperation of characters to achieve their goals.

In Polanski's *Macbeth*, the murder of King Duncan sends the crown spinning across the floor, symbolizing social chaos. Identify one play in which murder is central to the plot and establish how the film-maker has established the importance of the murder by the use of visual symbolism. Discuss the success of the scene in setting the tone of the film for the action that follows.

Childbirth and Early Survival

Juliet is the only surviving child from her parents' marriage—which helps to explain their reactions to Paris. Lady Macbeth speaks of the child to whom she has "given suck" as she works herself up to the murder of Duncan. (But no child is referred to elsewhere, so perhaps it has died; this might explain why she is so bitter.) Hamlet seems to be the only child of his father though we do not know how many times Hamlet senior may have married (one reason for Glenn Close to be the same age as Mel Gibson in the Zeffirelli version).

Early childhood diseases, death in childbirth and stillbirth are not dwelt on in Shakespeare's play-texts but they are commonly mentioned and form one argument for the marriage of very young women to older men. Shakespeare appears to have discussed this matter in a number of plays, suggesting that women should be older before they marry.

Use your research into Shakespeare's life and marriage to suggest why this should be a recurring theme in play-texts where there is no other motive for their appearance.

Satires, Spoofs, and Commercial Cinema

Shakespeare's play-texts have become increasingly popular subjects for film during the past thirty years. The most recent series of film translations have covered the historics, comedies, and tragedies in a range of innovative ways, some more successfully than others.

Shakespeare in Love is a delightful representation of what, most likely, was not the origin of *Romeo and Juliet*. Instead, it suggests that Shakespeare was one of a number of producers, playwrights, and actors all seeking attention in Elizabethan London. It plausibly suggests that some of the famous lines, especially the insults, were everyday sayings. Most importantly, it provides its viewers with a romantically realistic context in which to read and hear Elizabethan text.

Discuss the importance of the commercialization of Shakespeare for the reading and interpretation of his play-texts. Identify the insights you have gained into Shakespeare's world from viewing *Shakespeare in Love*.

Just as Shakespeare collected his plots from history, from popular stories and from current events of his time, Shakespeare's play-texts have presented modern day film-makers with plots for films which explore the issues without clinging to the language, the poetry of the detail.

- *Forbidden Planet* provided a launching pad for translating *The Tempest* to outer space.
- *Joe Macbeth* brought *Macbeth* to America as a gangster.
- *Kiss Me Kate* became a musical version of *Taming of the Shrew* while *West Side Story* was the musical version of *Romeo and Juliet*.

- *Hamlet* went west in 1972 as *Johnny Hamlet.*
- *Henry IV* became *Chimes at Midnight* for Orson Welles
- *King Lear* went west and was modernized in *A Thousand Acres.*
- *China Girl* brought a Chinese Juliet to New York to meet her Italian Romeo in a mafia-dominated Little Italy.
- In *Prospero's Books*, Peter Greenaway threw a little Tempest to create a cinematic wonderland for the Duke of Milan's revenge and a showcase for John Gielgud's voice, not to mention large scenes of nudity for late-night TV.

What other translations or borrowings from Shakespeare's plays can you discover? Discuss the effectiveness of any of these you have the opportunity to view.

Use one of the Shakespearean plays you have studied to create a film scenario that would be appealing to a present-day audience. Make specific notes of the cuts you have made; the changes in time and place; any changes in relationships which help to enhance the plot or intensify the themes.

Chronology

The Plays	Date	Historical Events
	1564	Shakespeare was born
	1582	Shakespeare married Anne Hathaway
	1570	Pope Pius excommunicated Elizabeth of England
		Lord Mayor of London forbade public performance within the walls of the city
	1577	Francis Drake sailed around the world
	1584	Walter Raleigh sailed to America
	1587	Mary Stuart executed
	1588	Elizabeth crowned Queen
		Defeat of the Spanish Armada
		Christopher Marlowe completed *Doctor Faustus*
Henry VI, Part 2	1590-91	
Henry VI, Part 3		
Henry VI, Part 1	1591-92	
Richard III	1592-93	All public places closed because of plague epidemic
The Comedy of Errors		Christopher Marlow killed
Titus Andronicus	1593-94	Shakespeare established with Lord Chamberlain's Men as actor, playwright, and shareholder
The Taming of the Shrew		Death of Thomas Kyd
Two Gentlemen of Verona	1594-95	Irish uprising
Loves Labour's Lost		
Sir Thomas More		3-page addition to this play is only known example of Shakespeare's handwriting
Romeo and Juliet		Romeo and Juliet said to be inspired by a novel by Bandello
Richard II	1595-96	Death of Hamnet
A Midsummer Night's Dream		
King John	1596-97	
The Merchant of Venice		
Henry IV, Part 1	1597-98	
Henry IV, Part 2		
Henry V	1598-99	
Much Ado About Nothing		
Julius Caesar	1599-00	Globe Theatre opened
As You Like It		Essex's expedition to Ireland

Twelfth Night		
Hamlet	1600-01	Giodano Bruno, supporter of Copernicus's helio-centric theory, burned at the stake
The Merry Wives of Windsor		
Troilus and Cressida	1601-02	Essex's plot against Elizabeth discovered; Essex executed
All's Well That Ends Well	1602-03	Theatres closed for plague epidemic
		Death of Elizabeth
		Crowning of James I of England (James VI of Scotland)
		Shakespeare's company Of Lord Chamberlain's Men become The King's Men
Othello	1604-05	The Gunpowder Plot
Measure for Measure		
King Lear	1605-06	
Macbeth		
Anthony and Cleopatra	1606-07	Daughter Susanna married
Coriolanus	1607-08	
Timon of Athens		
Pericles	1608-09	King's Men purchase Blackfriars Theatre
		Publication of the Sonnets
Cymbeline	1609-10	Shakespeare retired to Stratford
The Winter's Tale	1610-11	
The Tempest	1611-12	
Henry VIII	1612-13	Firing of a cannon in Henry VIII burnt the Globe Theatre down
	1616	April 23: Death of Shakespeare
	1623	"First Folio" published

To locate the plays with reference to historical events and to consider them in terms of development, we have provided a chronology developed from the works of T.W. Baldwin (1927) and E.K. Chambers (1923) as they have been affirmed by the editors of the Oxford edition of the complete works, Stanley Wells and Gary Taylor.

A range of dates has been attributed to most of the plays in this selection. These dates have been identified by scholars from manuscripts and records of the times—not all of which are, themselves, accurately dated. In addition, as Baldwin observes, some of them were not noted on their initial presentation (and some may have undergone name changes) but were later refined.

We recognize that some scholars disagree with these chronologies, but suggest that it is useful for students of Shakespeare, and of history, to abe able to consider, and even debate, the plays in a feasible developmental sequence. In support of this approach, we have included major personal or historical events against the years suggested for the initial performances of the plays.

References

Film

Apocalyse Now (1979), director Francis Ford Coppolla.
Army Intelligence (1994), director Penny Marshall.
Ben Hur (1959), director William Wyler.
Braveheart (1995), director Mel Gibson.
Broken Lance (1954), director Edward Dmytryck.
Bullitt (1968), director Peter Yates.
Chimes at Midnight (1966), director Orson Welles.
China Girl (1987), director Abel Ferrara.
Citizen Kane (1941), director Orson Welles.
Cleopatra (1963), director Joseph L. Mankiewicz.
Clueless (1995), director Amy Heckerling.
The Dresser (1983), director Peter Yates.
Elizabeth (1998), director Shekhar Kapur.
Forbidden Planet (1956), director Fred M Wilcox.
Goldfinger (1964), director Guy Hamilton.
The Good, the Bad, and the Ugly (1966), director Sergio Leone.
The Goodbye Girl (1977), director Herbert Ross.
Hamlet (1948), director Lawrence Olivier.
Hamlet (1969), director Tony Richardson.
Hamlet (1991), director Franco Zeffirelli.
Hamlet (1996), director Kenneth Branagh.
Hamlet Goes Business (1987), director Aki Kaurismäki.
Henry V (1944), director Laurence Olivier.
Henry V (1989), director Kenneth Branagh.
The House of Bernarda Alba (1987), director Mario Camus.
Joe Macbeth (1955), director Ken Hughes.
Johnny Hamlet (1972), director Enzo G. Castellari.
Julius Caesar (1953), director Joseph L. Mankiewicz.
Julius Caesar (1969), director Stuart Burge.
Julius Caesar (1978), director Herbert Wise.
Jurassic Park (1993), director Stephen Spielberg.
King Lear (1953), directors Peter Brook and Andrew McCullough.

King Lear (1969), director Peter Brook.

King Lear (1982), director Jonathan Miller.

King Lear (1984), director Michael Elliott.

King Lear (1987), director Jean-Luc Godard.

Kiss Me Kate (1953), director George Sidney.

Last Action Hero (1993), director John McTiernan.

Lethal Weapon (1987), director Richard Donner.

Looking for Richard (1996), director Al Pacino.

Macbeth (1972), director Roman Polanski.

Macbeth (1948), director Orson Welles.

The Magnificent Seven (1960), director John Sturges.

Men of Respect (1990), director William Reilly.

A Midsummer Night's Dream (1936), directors Max Reinhardt and William Dieterle.

A Midsummer Night's Dream (1981), director Elijah Moshinsky.

A Midsummer Night's Dream (1996), director Adrian Noble.

A Midsummer Night's Dream (1999), director Michael Hoffman.

A Midsummer Night's Dream (n.d.), director Celestino Coronado.

Much Ado About Nothing (1993), director Kenneth Branagh.

Othello (1951), director Orson Welles.

Othello (1965), director Stuart Burge.

Othello (1986), director Franco Zeffirelli.

Othello(1995), director Oliver Parker.

Platoon (1986), director Oliver Stone.

Peter's Friends (1992), director Kenneth Branagh.

Prospero's Books (1991), director Peter Greenaway.

Pulp Fiction (1994), director Quentin Tarantino.

The Purple Rose of Cairo (1984), director Woody Allen.

Ran (1985), director Akiro Kurosawa.

Richard III (1955), director Lawrence Olivier.

Richard III (1983), director Jane Howell.

Richard III (1996), directors John Loncraine and Ian McKellen.

Romeo and Juliet (1929), director George Cukor.

Romeo and Juliet (1954), director Renato Castellani.

Romeo and Juliet (1968), director Franco Zeffirelli.

Romeo and Juliet (1997), director Baz Luhrmann.

Rosencrantz and Guildenstern Are Dead (1990), director Tom Stoppard.

Scream (1996), director Wes Craven.

Seven (1995), director David Fincher.

The Seven Samurai (1954), director Akiro Kurosawa.

Shaft (1971), director Gordon Parks.

Shakespeare in Love (1998), director John Madden.

Spartacus (1960), director Stanley Kubrick.

The Taming of the Shrew (1967), director Franco Zeffirelli.

The Taming of the Shrew (1929), director Sam Taylor.

Ten Things I Hate About You (1999), director Gil Junger.

The Terminator (1984), director James Cameron.

A Thousand Acres (1997), director Jocelyn Moorhouse.

Throne of Blood (1957), director Akiro Kurosawa.

Titanic (1997), director James Cameron.

Titus (1999), director Julie Taymor.

Top Gun (1986), director Tony Scott.

Twelfth Night (1980), director John Gorrie.

Twelfth Night (1986), director Neil Armfield.

Twelfth Night (1988), directors Kenneth Branagh and Paul Kafno.

Twelfth Night (1996), director Trevor Nunn.

The Wars of the Roses: Richard III (1990), director Michael Bogdanov.

West Side Story (1961), directors Robert Wise and Jerome Robins.

The Wizard of Oz (1925), director Larry Semon.

Text

Baldwin, T.W. (1927) *Organisation and Personnel of the Shakespearean Company.* Princeton, 229-283.

Bate, J. (1997) *The Genius of Shakespeare.* London: Picador.

Boose, Lynda E, and Burt, Richard. (1997) *Shakespeare, The Movie: Popularising the Plays on Film, TV and Video.* London/New York: Routledge.

Brakhage, Stan. (1977) *Film Biographies.* Berkeley, California: Turtle Island.

Brockbank, Philip. (1988) *Players of Shakespeare 1.* Cambridge: Cambridge University Press.

Bulman, J.C., and Coursen, H.R., eds. (1988) *Shakespeare on Television.* Hanover, NH: University Press of New England.

Chambers, E.K. (1923) *The Elizabethan Stage.* Vol. 1. Oxford: Oxford University Press, 270–271.

Chong, Denise. (1996). *The Concubine's Daughter.* UK: Penguin.

Collick, John. (1989) *Shakespeare, Cinema and Society.* Manchester: Manchester University Press.

Coursen, Herbert E. (1997) *Teaching Shakespeare with Film and Television: A Guide.* Westport, CT: Greenwood Press.

Craig, Hardin, ed. (1961) *The Complete Works of Shakespeare.* New York: Scott Foresman.

Davies, Anthony, and Wells, Stanley, eds. (1994) *Shakespeare and the Moving Image: The Plays on Film and Television.* Cambridge: Cambridge University Press.

Davis, James E. and Salomone, Ronald E. (1993) *Teaching Shakespeare Today: Practical Approaches and Productive Strategies.* Urbana, IL: National Council of Teachers of English.

Durrant, Calvin. (1996) *To Prove a Villain: A Workshop Approach to Richard III.* Revised edition. Sydney: St Clair Press.

Eco, Umberto. 1979. *The Role of the Reader: Explorations in the Semiotics of Texts.* Bloomington, IN: Indiana University Press.

French, Jackie. (2000) *Lady Dance.* Sydney: Angus & Robertson.

Friedlander, Larry. (1988) "The Shakespeare Project: Experiments in Multimedia Education." *Academic Computing,* 2(7): 20–29; 66–68. (Summary in *The Writing Notebook: Creative Word Processing in the Classroom,* 8(4): 4–6 [1991])

Griffin, C.W. (1989) "Teaching Shakespeare on Video." *English Journal,* 77 (7): 40–43.

Hall, Sandra. *Sydney Morning Herald* 21/1/97.

Hunter, Evan. (1997). *Me and Hitch.* London: Faber.

Kittredge, G.L. (1940) *The Tragedy of King Lear.* London: Ginn.

Loehlin, James. (1997) " 'Top of the World, Ma': Richard III and the Cinematic Convention." In Lynda Boose and Richard Burt, eds., *Shakespeare: the Movie.* London: Routledge.

Mallick, D. (1984) *How Tall is This Ghost, John?* Adelaide: Australian Association of Teachers of English.

Manvell, Roger. (1979) *Shakespeare and the Film.* South Brunswick, NJ: Barnes

McLean, Andrew M. (1980) *Shakespeare: Annotated Bibliographies and Media Guide for Teachers.* Urbana, IL: National Council of Teachers of English.

McKellen, Ian. (1996) *William Shakespeare's Richard III—A Screenplay.* London: Doubleday.

McMurtry, Jo. (1994) *Shakespeare Films in the Classroom: A Descriptive Guide.* New York: Archon Books.

Olivier, Lawrence. (1982) *Confessions of an Actor.* London: Weidenfeld and Nicolson.

Parsons, Keith, and Mason, Pamela, eds. (1995) *Shakespeare in Performance.* London: Salamander Books.

Partridge, E. (1960) *Shakespeare's Bawdy*. New York: E.P. Dutton.

Pepper, Frank S. (1990) *20th Century Anecdotes*. London: Sphere.

Rothwell, Kenneth S., and Melzer, Annabelle Henkin. (1990) *Shakespeare on Screen: An International Filmography and Videography*. New York/London: Neal-Schuman.

Spurgeon, Caroline F.E. (1935/1965) *Shakespeare's Imagery and What It Tells Us*. Cambridge: Cambridge University Press.

Sterne, Richard L. (1967) *John Gielgud Directs Richard Burton in Hamlet: A Journal of Rehearsals*. New York: Random House.

Tuska, Jon. (1991) *Encounters with Film-makers: Eight Career Studies*. New York: Greenwood.

Willis, Susan. (1991) *The BBC Shakespeare Plays: Making the Televised Canon*. Chapel Hill, NC: University of North Carolina Press.

Willinsky, John, and Bedard, J. (1989) *The Fearful Passage: Romeo and Juliet in the High School, A Feminist Perspective*. Ottawa: Canadian Council of Teachers of English.

Contributors

Dr. Neil E. Béchervaise is a professor in English Education at the University of Sydney, Australia, where he has achieved the Award for Excellence in Teaching. He has been a visiting professor at the University of British Columbia, Canada. A published poet, his research on reading response and the use of text in multicultural classrooms is incorporated into an increasing number of major Australian texts.

Dr. Joe Belanger is a professor and deputy head of the Department of Language and Literary Education at the University of British Columbia, where he teaches courses in English methods, technical communication, and curriculum studies. He is a former president of the Canadian Council of Teachers of English and editor of several language education journals.

Bill Davison lectures in the Department of Language and Literacy Education at the University of British Columbia where he teaches English methods and foundations courses in the teacher education program. Formerly an English teacher and department head in Vancouver schools, Bill has also served as president of the Vancouver Secondary Teachers' Association.

Jodie McFadden trained as an English teacher at the University of Sydney and now teaches high school English with the Queensland Education Department.

Dr. Dennis Robinson is a professor in English Education at the University of Sydney. Author of a number of texts in literary criticism and former president of the English Association, he is a committed reader and teacher-educator whose research explores the dynamic between author, text, and reader development.

Sarah Tainton trained as an English teacher at the University of Sydney and now teaches high school English with the New South Wales Education Department.

Ken Watson has been a visiting professor at the University of British Columbia and is a former professor in English Education at the University of Sydney. He now directs, and writes for St Clair Press, an Australian publishing house specializing in quality resources for English education.

Index